UNFOLDING

UNFOLDING

THE
PERPETUAL SCIENCE OF
YOUR SOUL'S WORK

JULIA MOSSBRIDGE

NEW WORLD LIBRARY
NOVATO, CALIFORNIA

New World Library
14 Pamaron Way
Novato, California 94949

Front cover design by Mary Ann Casler
Text design and typography by Mary Ann Casler

Library of Congress Cataloging-in-Publication Data

Mossbridge, Julia
Unfolding : the perpetual science of your soul's work / Julia
Mossbridge.
p.   cm.
ISBN 1-57731-193-0 (pbk. : alk. paper)
1. Spiritual life. 2. Self-realization — Religious aspects. I. Title.
BL624 .M6756 2002
291.4'4—dc21   2001005937

First Printing, February 2002
ISBN 1-57731-193-0
Printed in Canada on acid-free paper
Distributed to the trade by Publishers Group West

10 9 8 7 6 5 4 3 2 1

This is for everyone.
May we all be more like ourselves.

CONTENTS

FOREWORD

When I think of Work, I think of something that is much larger than the jobs we happen to hold. I read once that our work is the role we play in the unfolding of the universe. As Matthew Fox wrote, "work comes from the inside out; work is the expression of our soul, our inner being. It is unique to the individual; it is creative."[1] My ultimate vision is of individuals who are full of life and joy, and who then take that life and joy and unleash them through service to their communities or wider society. Their service might be through the production of goods and services in business; through administration in government; through teaching; or through some other means, but whatever it is, it incorporates their vision and joy. Who we are, what we believe, and what we long for — all these need to be integrated into the work we do and the role we play in our families and communities.

Unfolding is an important contribution to that process of unleashing life and joy. I am someone who is very much driven by my heart — I am doing the work I love and believe in. It is so very clear to me that I could be doing nothing else than what I am doing. And so a book to assist me in clarifying my passion and purpose and my plan for bringing my gift to the world initially seemed to me important, but not something that I needed myself. How mistaken I was.

1. Matthew Fox, *The Reinvention of Work* (San Francisco: HarperCollins, 1995).

Each chapter and each segment had something immensely valuable to offer. I felt that in developing a deeper conscious-ness around what my nature and gift actually are, and in being supported in making (or re-affirming) conscious choices around my path, I was in fact being assisted in harnessing my personal fire, coming out of the experience (and experiments!) of the book more clear and ready to continue on my way. And so I would venture that this book is both for those who think they know where they're going and how, as well as for those who are still actively seeking direction.

What it brought me, even as I am on my way, was an active reminder that it is not so much about exactly where one is going, but much more about how best to get there. This may sound paradoxical at first. I recall what a good friend of mine once said, "I don't know where I'm going, but I know how to get there." She felt very comfortable in that knowing. What knowing was that? I suspect it was knowing quite clearly the best ways for her to move in the world (the ways that made her happy and brought light to others), how to listen to her inner voices and follow them, how to connect with and relate to people by offering them what was uniquely her. Exactly where this would take her was an ongoing discovery, though this is not to say that she just let fate determine the outcome. Of course she had goals, but she knew that the path, and the way she walked it, were more important, and that the specific goals might shift as things change, as they do. I think Julia's book holds a little of that spirit.

Who are you? What fires you up? How might you live into that more fully?

An upward stretching movement. I wish to be an upward stretching movement. I wish to be a conduit for life, a channel, feeling the energy stream through me. I wish to be like the bird gliding in the wind, and I wish to be like the tree growing into its own unique gnarled and wild identity.

I wish to be like the runner hot with sweat, aware of her
heart beating, and feeling life pulsating through her. I wish
to be like the project group that comes together in a sense of
awe as creativity strikes in its midst. I wish to learn the tune
of life, and sing its song, in all its fullness.

Julia's book both helps one delve into the personal levels of
nature and purpose, and also continues moving on to the important aspect of sharing and working with others. I appreciated
this greatly — how it spans wide, yet goes deep into each aspect
of unfolding our Selves. It is not a navel-gazing book set to keep
people introspecting. Of course any journey starts with recon-
necting to Self, and this one goes there. It also helps take us further out into the world with the gifts we each have to offer.

It is clear that the book is written by a scientist — a won-
derfully loving and humorous one at that. I thoroughly enjoyed
the design of the experiments that are sprinkled throughout the
book, helping the reader really engage in an experiment of Self,
and further on also including others. The meeting in Julia of
the truth-seeking scientist and the woman who seeks to tune
into her soul's work brings us an incredible, important gift. She
has built a bridge between our still rational mechanistic world
and the new perception that is emerging: a biological view of
the universe, where we, like all other beings, are participants in
the continuous unfolding of life and creation.

I co-founded a network called Pioneers of Change, a global
learning community of committed young change agents who
come together to connect with our deeper values and ideals and
to generate innovative solutions to challenges faced in our
communities and organizations. At the core of the network is
the commitment of its members to live by five basic but profound principles:

To be yourself
To do what matters

To start now
To engage with others, and
To never stop asking questions.

Julia's book provides an incredible tool to help us support each other in exploring more deeply what each of these principles means practically to each one of us. What does it mean for me to be myself? To do what matters to me? To start now? To engage fruitfully and openly with others? And underlying the book itself is the need to be constantly asking questions to take us further down the path we have each chosen to tread.

I am driven by a greater vision for how our societies could work, and how we as people could be with each other. I have realized that it is a drive that starts from a very personal place.

Do you think things could be different?

Dare we ask ourselves the question? What might we do, and what might we create, if we followed a deeper call?

Thank you, Julia; and to you, the person, reading this, welcome to the journey of unfolding.

MARIANNE KNUTH
Harare, Zimbabwe, November 7, 2001
pioneersofchange.net

PREFACE
An Invitation to the Reader

I magine you are at a party where people avoid small talk. Someone approaches you and bluntly asks who you are, what your work in life is, and exactly how you are actively engaged in healing the world. Would you have an answer? Could you tell them about your nature, your purpose, and your plan for bringing your particular genius to the world? If you could, then you don't need this book.

Or would you stammer and wonder to yourself what the answer might be? Or might you know the answer but not know how to implement it? Then, like most of us, you are ready for unfolding — bringing your whole self to the world. Unfolding is not a goal but a continuous state of transformation that is possible for every one of us. We are meant to unfold, and we are made to learn how. But we have to choose it.

In every moment, we have this choice. We can choose to bring forward what is hidden within us, or we can choose to ignore our gifts. If we choose the possibilities that live inside us, we find joy, true power, and healing peace. If we make the other choice — if we resist our own unfolding — we damage ourselves. This damage manifests as depression, lack of community, and disease.

This book provides an experimental path to revealing the mysteries within you and using them to repair the world. And that's all it provides. I am not a psychologist, minister, or rabbi. I cannot draw on the status of a famous performer or speaker. And yet neither they nor I can tell you what is inside you. That is your job. If you choose your unfolding, this book will become a partner in your work.

ACKNOWLEDGMENTS

Thanks first to the teachers who taught me to love my soul as well as my mind. In chronological order: God, Mom, Dad, Jenny, Grand-mère, Mrs. Ruzich, Mrs. Thomas, Karen Martin, Rita Schulien, the Libertyville Gang, Gen Churchill, Michelle Trask, Linda Shih, Mrs. Lowey, Mr. Neumark, Ms. Papp, Mr. Spooner, Mr. Strode, Gale Granbert-Roman, Steve Tomasic, Dan Hosken, Amy Evans, Mary Beth Thornton, Dr. Braford, Dr. Loose, Dr. Tamkun, Lee Honigberg, Dr. Gumbiner, Dr. Dallman, Dr. Fields, Dr. Morgan, Adam Mossbridge, George Wilkinson, Joan Autio, Kathie Wickstrand, Kay Henderson, Dr. Stern, Bill Levin, Elon Cameron, Laura Goldman, Mike Kaufman, Dr. Kraus, Dr. Wright, Joseph Mossbridge, everyone in Humans in Science, all the Friday-morning moms, the Pioneers of Change listserv folks, Matt Fitzgerald, Jeanette Ortiz, God....

I am amazed at and grateful for the vision and patience of Georgia Hughes, my editor at New World Library. She was always right, especially when she liked my final draft. Also thanks to everyone at New World for picking such a beautiful and energetic cover design and for taking my opinions seriously. I would not have found Georgia or New World without my agent, Katie Boyle, at Veritas, nor would I have the courage to rewrite the text without her constant belief in me.

Thank you Katie, the most down-to-earth and supportive of agents!

For feedback, discussions, contributions, and guidance on the book itself, I thank (again in chronological order): Sullivan Hester, John Hagstrand, Dori Conn, Kay Henderson, Wayne Teasdale, Sonia Choquette, Gay Hendricks, Dr. Yount, Mom, Karen Martin, Bill Levin, Jennifer Armstrong, Rebecca Armstrong, Connie Scanlon of Bogfire Productions, Carolyn Carney, Michelle Trask, Amir Gharaat, Greg Newman, all my coaching clients, my partner Adam Garret Walters, Stephanie Baselice, Polly Washburn, Marianne Knuth, Mike Kaufman, Ed Shea, Laurie Pentell at Sageheart, everyone in the Unfolding.org circle (especially Paolina A., Kim T., Clayton G.-F., and Barrett B.), Rabbi Rosen, Kay Silva, Amy Kipfer, and everyone in the Unfolding workshop series (especially Terry T., Michelle C., Ola J., and Todd F.).

Thanks also to the staff of the Women's Place Resource Center, the Eleanor House, Borders bookstore in Evanston, and the Ridgeville Park District for allowing me to create and facilitate my workshops in their space.

Thanks to my sister, Jenny, for being a supportive and understanding presence in my life. Thanks to my son, Joseph, for strengthening my voice and for taking long naps during the week before the first deadline, and to Adam for being my biggest fan.

A special thanks to my parents — Dad, Mom, and Karen — who have always seen and loved the brightness in my soul.

INTRODUCTION

My father looks just like an Amish farmer, but he's actually a theoretical physicist. When I was a kid and afraid to go up the creaky oak stairs in our dark and ancient farmhouse, my father would say, "Do it as an experiment. Climb up the stairs and see if you get eaten by monsters. I'll clap when you get to the top." So I climbed the stairs, sweat pouring into my pajamas. The idea of turning what I feared into an experiment made me feel like a scientist, an explorer.

When I was growing up, my father and I investigated everything from the mechanics of toothbrushing to the source of the mysterious reflections in our wobbly-glass windows. Our photo-acoustic solar-powered bicycle/sound machine won first prize at the eighth-grade science fair (though my sister was miffed that I had borrowed her bicycle). In high school I fell in love with the movements of tiny molecules in chemistry class, and when I got to college, I fell in love with the complexity of the human brain. After college I joined a competitive neuroscience Ph.D. program and became interested in stress, pain, and the physiological connections between them. In every experimental venture, I continued to feel like an intrepid explorer of the universe, revealing beautiful truths that lie just beneath the surface of things.

Yet after I took my qualifying exam and received my master's degree, I felt like something was missing. My days were a blur of wires, electrodes, and rat brains. I was exploring as usual, and yet I didn't feel right. At a scientific conference in the Netherlands, I saw some birds flying in a pattern that I interpreted to mean that I should take a break from science for a while. At that point, I was so desperate for some perspective that I could have seen bubblegum on the sidewalk and made the same interpretation. After I got home, I announced that I was going to leave the graduate program and discover my soul's work.

I became a radio talk-show host, personal coach, software tester, energy healer, workshop leader, and Web designer. I struggled for a while over whether to become a rabbi or return to the life of a scientist. Finally I found myself falling back in love with science and returning to graduate school. But I could only return to my path as a scientist when I saw that in science I was doing the same work that I did in every other job I had tried: I discovered hidden truths and brought them to the world.

When I looked at things this way, I saw that science and unfolding can be seen as different ways to use the same process. The process entails answering these three essential questions:

1. What is the hidden truth?
2. How can I partner with the Universe to bring it out?
3. How will bringing it out heal the world?

When we enter into our unfolding, we become the scientists of our souls. Just because we aren't faraway galaxies, stem cells, or retroviruses does not mean we aren't worthy of scientific exploration. And just because science can seem impersonal, cold, and irrelevant doesn't mean it actually is. After all, we created science, so we can use it however we like. If we embrace the tools of open experimentation and apply them to ourselves, we can discover the work we are here to do.

HOW THIS BOOK WORKS

This book has two jobs. One is to provide a structure for the discovery and enhancement of your life's work. The other job is to help you learn how you unfold, to make conscious to you how your transformation works. This second job is maybe even more important than the first — because if you can learn about your particular way of bringing your gifts to the world, then you can apply this awareness to your future unfolding. You will be more effective, focused, and playful each time you engage in your unfolding. So my hope is that you will travel your path with a dual purpose: to bring yourself to fruition and to observe and discover how you do it.

This book consists of three parts. In the first ("Discover"), you will discover your nature and purpose. In the second ("Master"), you will learn how to navigate your path by developing and deepening your partnership with God. In the third part ("Share"), you will share your gifts, using them to create positive change in yourself and the world. At the end of each of the three parts, I have included what I call Soul Maps. The Soul Maps are meant to provide a place for you to integrate, synthesize, and make practical your discoveries. Finally, the epilogue invites you to consider your future unfolding.

ABOUT GOD

I see God as the love that moves in us, through us, and beyond us: a very abstract concept. But when I am in relationship with God, it feels more like I'm in relationship with a person than with a concept. As a result, I write about God as a person. I try to use both masculine and feminine terms, and every so often, I replace *God* with other words like *Nature, Love, Spirit,* and *Universe.* I do this mostly to remind myself that there can be more than one name for God. I encourage you to replace my words with the words that work for you and for your view of God.

At the back of the book (starting on page 115), you'll find a wealth of tools that you can use to supplement your work. I wanted to call this section "Chemistry Set" in an attempt to evoke the excitement that I felt as a kid when I opened my box full of mysterious and colorful vials. However, a good number of people never really felt that kind of excitement about chemistry sets. So instead, I call it the "Laboratory Tool Kit." The tools are neatly divided into their related chapters, so you don't have to search for a tool that addresses a particular concept. I invite you to flip to the "Laboratory Tool Kit" and play with the tools there whenever you need some extra inspiration in your unfolding work.

In each chapter, I discuss how to work with a difficult emotion or experience that can help you move forward in the work of that chapter. I call these "shadow tools," because feelings like shame, fear, sadness, anger are often thought of as negative experiences. And while it's true that these feelings are often unpleasant to have, as you learn how to use them they can become tools for your unfolding.

Each chapter also contains a selected meditation, practice, and/or ritual that you can use to deepen your experience of the work. Meditations bring your unfolding work into your daily life. Practices help you learn new habits. And rituals are for getting a really visceral experience of the work.

At the end of each chapter I have designed an experiment that summarizes the ideas in the chapter. These experiments are the heart of the work. When you do them, let yourself do them fairly. Don't walk into the lab, smash the test tubes, and proclaim that the experiment didn't work. Do the experiments with an open heart, knowing that whatever you find is what you are meant to see.

The work is self-paced; you can use the guidelines at the end of each chapter to decide whether you are ready to move on. But also know that the work is cumulative — if you don't feel quite ready, take the leap anyway. The next chapter will reinforce what you have already done and will expand on it.

The book is also designed so you can customize it to your needs. You can use the meditations, practices, rituals, and experiments from the chapters, select alternative tools from the "Laboratory Tool Kit," or invent your own. *Your unfolding is your responsibility.* Once you commit to it, you have to find the tools that work for you, whether or not they come from this book.

I have struggled with and refined the ideas I present, and I think they are as close to true as I can get them. But some ideas may be wrong. Or they may not be right for you. Even so, I encourage you to entertain them. A favorite mentor of mine speaks of entertaining an idea in this way: "Ask the idea in for tea, talk a while, and only then decide how you feel about it."

After entertaining the idea you may find that you disagree with it. If so, challenge yourself to describe in detail the alternative that works for you. For example, at one point I claim that we have two basic fears about working with God. Let's say that after entertaining this idea you disagree with it. Let's say you think there is only one basic fear, or one hundred. Great! Just challenge yourself to describe why the "two-fears" theory doesn't work for you. As you do, you'll make more important discoveries about yourself than I could ever make for you.

Because your unfolding is experimental, you'll need a place to record your discoveries. This is your Unfolding Notebook. In your notebook, you will record your fears and desires, your confusion and clarity, your setbacks and leaps. Your Unfolding Notebook can be an archival-quality sketchbook or a spiral-bound seventy-nine-cent deal. In my workshops, some people get really into it and draw pictures, paste images, and write odes to their unfolding. Others like a simpler approach and just take notes on their observations. The point is to get a notebook and use it.

If you are afraid that keeping your Unfolding Notebook will be too much work, take too much time, and make you feel uncomfortable or incompetent, then listen up! You see, your fears are misplaced. The work will become joyful before too long, and then it won't feel like work at all. As for time, it will take at most five minutes a day once you have read a chapter and thirty minutes total for the work in the Soul Maps. As for feeling uncomfortable or incompetent, what I can tell you is that as you create your Unfolding Notebook, you will feel enlivened and brilliant instead.

You can read through this book without keeping your notebook. You can get a lot of good information that way. I can tell you, "Look! There are beautiful things inside you!" and you can nod your head. Sure. But to have a visceral experience of this beauty, to know it with a full heart, you need to do some work.

Most of the people who asked to "road test" this book told me how scared they were. If you are scared, this is good. It means you realize that what you are in for is powerful, irreversible, and profound. There is nothing more frightening than choosing to do the work you came here to do. Except not doing it.

Sometimes unfolding feels enlivening, joyful, and transcendent. And sometimes we'd rather not do it at all. It seems like unfolding should be easy because we're built to do it, and every so often it does come easily. Yet at other times it can feel trying, because we aren't taught to pay attention to our own experience. That's why the title of this book is not *Unfolding: Your Soul's Work in Seven Easy Steps*. A more accurate title (though it probably would have been rejected by the marketing department) would be *Unfolding: Your Soul's Work in an Infinite Number of Sometimes-Easy, Sometimes-Hard, but Always-Deepening Steps*.

This work isn't about being perfect, reaching some ideal, or joining a "club of the transformed." It's not about being anyone other than who you already are. It is a method for joyously discovering, polishing, and integrating the jewels of your unfolding, the gifts that you are meant to bring to the world.

Here is your soul's work: to discover what's inside you, to bring your discoveries out, to help repair the world. And then to begin again. Commit to doing your work well and with diligence. Commit to being truthful about what really moves you and what makes you cringe. Commit to finding your hidden truths, knowing them, and bringing them out for all to see.

- We have gifts inside us that can be developed and brought out to heal ourselves and the world. This is unfolding, and it is what we are meant to do.
- Unfolding needs our love, time, and conscious participation.
- This book offers a path to discovery, but you are the only one who knows your gifts and how best to share them with the world.
- When you are unfolding you are in partnership with God.
- We are never done unfolding.

 UNFOLDING

A sprout grows damp under the earth. It pokes through weak mud, following the light, gently leaning toward nourishment. The sprout unfurls. With its flesh, it creates stalks, leaves, flowers, and fruits. It flourishes through a growing season, withers with the frost, falls limp and crisp under leaves. Insects come, they decompose, and the earth is nourished. With each moment the growth of this plant unfolds, following an innate design.

Likewise, each of us contains a blueprint for the continual discovery of our true nature and purpose. Our blueprint has always been with us; part of us already knows its secrets. But there is still a mystery to this blueprint. The mystery is not only what it contains but how it will unfold. If we allow our blueprint to unfold in its way, carefully encouraging its movements, time and nourishment will foster the birth of an exceptional being.

As you work through each chapter, know there is no right way, no strange way, no stuck way, no perfect way for your unfolding to happen. Unfolding is an experimental mystery school taught by your spirit. It is the unique science of your particular soul. Allow your experience. Let it grow, breathe, and live in love, time, and nourishment.

A part of us has known our whole lives how the human spirit grows. This part holds ancient wisdom, ingrained in our hearts. There is another part of us, more scared and much younger, who is taking this journey for the first time.

Unfolding is a union of these two parts: the wise and the young, the parent and child. Our work needs both. The parent will nurture the development of the child; the child will teach the parent. This work is created for both parent and child, the parts inside us and the whole they will become.

Welcome to your unfolding.

UNFOLDING

PART ONE
DISCOVER

CHAPTER ONE

NATURE

CHAPTER GOAL:

To remember how to
be who you are

I have beautiful lips. They are large and succulent and red. I don't wear lipstick, because I don't need to. My lips are like pomegranate halves; even the most reluctant passersby stare at their ruby ripeness. My lips are gravity defying; their beauty sends falling stars back up into the sky.

What happens when you read this? Some will flip to the back cover to check out my lips. Many of you will be embarrassed for me. What pride I must have to speak so highly of my lips! They're probably not so great, you might think. (Of course, you'd be wrong.) When someone sings their own praises, we have a knee-jerk shaming response — a blush, a snicker, or a correction. When I was nine years old, I caught a glimpse of my lips in a mirror and told my mother, "I think I have a beautiful mouth." She immediately responded, "Don't say those things; you might get a big head."

To be fair to my mother, I told her this story recently, and she couldn't believe she would say something so thoughtless. But she did, and she said it automatically. She had fully absorbed all the messages that say we'd better forget our own light. That we'd better hide our own beauty so we can remake ourselves into another image — the image we think other people want to see, a strange picture that often doesn't resemble us at all.

As we grow up and learn to hide our light, we soon forget our uniqueness. But even underneath the new picture we've laid on top of ourselves, we can see something shining. We can start to ask questions, to know the source of light inside us — the source that was in hiding.

When I looked it up in the dictionary, I found that the word *nature* has two meanings: the natural world and our natures as individual human beings. As in, "Don't mess with Mother Nature" and, "I can't help being a geek; it's my nature." The work in this chapter encompasses both meanings: It is about discovering the beauty of the universe that is expressed through who we are.

RULES OF THE SOURCE

I once worked with a man who often quoted self-help books. He kind of drove me crazy, because he was always talking about how to be himself, but he would rarely *be* it. He seemed uncomfortable inside his own skin — always trying to impress others with skills or personality traits that weren't quite genuine. It's like he had all this "spiritual makeup" hiding his true beauty. Yet every so often he would let his nature shine; little bits of light would escape. When this happened, he was beautiful and a delight to be with. Each time he let a little light out, he seemed to relax. It's as if being himself fueled his capacity to be himself some more.

There is a source of energy that lives in us. We have stored love in this brilliant source, and it wants to come out into the world. Focusing on that place of love is the shortest path to healing the world. This source is not your nature; it is the place from which your nature shines. If this source is a star, your nature is its light. When you choose to let your source shine, you can feel its heat warming you from within, and your nature finding its way out into the world.

For most of us, two beliefs get in the way of letting our source shine: the belief that we are not allowed to let it shine (it's not good enough, it's too overwhelming, it detracts from others, and so on) and the belief that if we shine, we'll run out of light. Both these beliefs work against us, reducing our ability to fully express our nature. So we need to remind ourselves of what we once knew: the rules of our source.

The first rule is that it is okay to shine. In fact, it is what we're meant to do. Why else would we have this brightness in us, if it weren't allowed to shine? The second rule is as we use our light, we don't lose it. Instead, we create more of it. We are like stars that need the heat created from our burning to support more burning. Expressing your nature gives you the energy you need to keep expressing your nature. Both rules are crucial, but it's not so easy to follow them. In fact, this whole chapter is devoted to making the transition from squelched light to beaming star.

How Do You Shine?

I love personality tests. And I am not alone. Millions of people will answer questions about themselves to discover someone else's definition of who they really are. But we already know whether we like to be the center of attention or move to the edge of a room. We know whether we'd prefer to read a book or act in a play. So why do we take these tests? Because it's comfort-

> HOW TO TELL WHEN YOU ARE EXPRESSING YOUR NATURE
>
> • You feel connected with yourself.
> • You have more energy.
> • You feel calm and alive.

ing to have someone else tell us that our personality is normal. It's also comforting (but wrong) to think our nature is unchanging and easy to define.

Since our nature is always evolving, we will never actually

get a definitive grasp on a single label that describes Who We Are. Fortunately, that's not what we're really after anyway. What we really want is not to *label* Who We Are, but to *be* who we are. We can't discover our nature and then keep that discovery with us forever. But we can discover how to best express who we are. This discovery we *can* keep forever.

How you can start is by noticing when you are shining. When you are expressing who you are you feel connected, energized, and calm. Once you start to notice yourself expressing your nature, you can get a brief glimpse of your nature in that moment. How are you shining? Are you like a star? A stream of sunlight? A million suns, up close? Are you a pulsar, rhythmically dancing in the sky? A quiet candle on a bookshelf?

When you let your light shine in exactly its own way, the world can see your beauty. Only your particular way will do; only the way that is true to your nature in this moment. No one else's way will work, and you can't use previous versions of yourself to substitute for your nature in this moment.

Rabbi Zusya of Hanipoli once said, "When I die, God will not ask me, 'Why weren't you more like Moses?' God will ask me, 'Why weren't you more like Zusya?'" The rest of the world needs your nature to shine so we can see the glory of the Universe. This is how important you are.

THE YES PRACTICE

GOAL: *To become open to exactly how your nature is expressing itself right now*

STEP ONE: *Say "yes" to your body.*

Close your eyes and breathe. Feel your whole body — everything. Feel the parts that are sore and the parts that are relaxed and free. Cuticles are not off-limits. As you feel each part, don't try to change it. Instead, just say "yes" to yourself, or even aloud.

STEP TWO: *Say "yes" to your mind.*

When thoughts, ideas, or feelings come up, don't try to name them or change them. Just say "yes." As you say "yes" to an idea or thought, know that this does not necessarily mean you agree with it. For example, if a part of you really wants to kill the cat, you can say "yes" to it — as in "yes, there is a part of me that really wants to kill the cat." But you don't need to act on any desires, images, or thoughts without making a conscious choice.

STEP THREE: *Feel your nature.*

As you continually say "yes" to whatever comes up, allow yourself to feel (not label) what it feels like when you are letting your nature be exactly as it is.

NOTE: At the end of each practice, meditation, ritual, or experiment you try, you might want to use your Unfolding Notebook to record how it worked for you. If you changed anything to make it work better, or if you replaced it with another practice entirely, make a note of that too.

SHAME: A SHADOW TOOL

A three-year-old boy is in the grocery store, shopping with his father. The entire trip he has been in the cart, legs over the side, quietly working on a knot bracelet. In the checkout line, when the bracelet is finished, he glows with pride. He shows his creation to his dad. His father picks it up without comment and asks the cashier if he can throw it in the garbage, thinking it's something his son found in his coat. The kid is crestfallen, his hard work ignored. Dad never knows the difference. One piece of this child's nature — a resourceful artist — has been unwittingly dismissed.

Most of us have had at least some experiences like this;

when they happen consistently, we feel shame about who we are. If this three-year-old is told that his creative efforts are worthless too many times, he'll hide his artistic nature. He'll decide that maybe his nature is ugly, invisible, or wrong. He'll create a version of himself that has no need for creativity, possibly becoming an art critic.

An acquaintance of mine from college was studying to be a social worker. She felt compelled to help other people, often to her own detriment. Yet she wasn't excited about any of her courses. As I learned more about her childhood, I could understand why. Her parents had told her she was selfish every time she wanted something that her disabled sister couldn't have — like ballet lessons or a bike. She became ashamed of the things she wanted to do, so she made herself into a completely selfless person. Once she realized what had happened, she began to discover her natural talents for dance. She combined dance with her social work background and became a movement therapist. Once she worked through her shame and understood that what she needed was not shameful, her nature took over by itself.

When we use it as a tool, shame offers at least two gifts. It shows us how our nature has been suppressed in the past, and it points us toward what we need so we can express our nature in the future. When my mother told me I was too proud of my lips, I burned with shame. I felt like I had made a bad mistake — how could I see such beauty in myself? But after a few years of pressed lips and fake smiles, I let myself remember that I was right. My lips are beautiful. And more important, who I am is a person who needs to be seen and appreciated.

THE SHAME MEDITATION

GOAL: *To identify your shame and let it tell*
you what your nature needs

For a few minutes, meditate on this statement: "My nature needs what I am ashamed that I need." Ask yourself these questions, writing your answers in your Unfolding Notebook:

What am I ashamed of?
What does this tell me about my past?
What can this help me know about my future?
What is one thing I can do, right now, to give my nature what it needs?

RESONANCE

I asked a friend to join me for an early-morning walk to take in birdsong, buses, and panhandlers and to talk about lofty ideas. But what I really wanted from our time together was to get sympathy from her. She and I had a mutual friend who I believed had wronged me. I wanted to tell my story and hear from her that he had been a real jerk.

Unfortunately, my plan backfired. I discovered that I had picked my friends too well. She explained how our mutual friend might have seen the situation, and she told me that I needed to talk with him. Her reaction may sound unsympathetic to some, but to me it was perfect. I feel at home with people who challenge me to see all sides of a story. I feel

> ### WHEN YOU ARE IN YOUR RESONANT ENVIRONMENT
>
> • you are constantly being refueled by it,
> • you find it easy to express your nature,
> • you find it difficult to block your source.

respected and loved with these kinds of people, because I know if someone else approached them to gossip about me, my friends would give equally compassionate advice. These people act as resonators for my nature. They are part of my resonant environment — the environment that most supports the expression of who I am.

Resonance is what you feel when someone is on your wavelength; you feel continuously energized, not drained. When you resonate with someone, it is easy to express who you are and difficult to hide your true nature. As children, we want to get this resonance mainly from our parents; as we grow older we also want it from our partners, our coworkers, and our friends. When we can't find it there, we look for it in increasingly bizarre places, such as cars, drugs, or television. We are desperate for resonance because we have a primal instinct — we are driven to support and reveal our nature.

It is so easy to block your nature that you need to consciously create an environment that will help remove those blocks. This is the first healing act we need to perform before we concern ourselves with healing the world. It is easy to let the lives of others who need us distract us from healing our own personal lives. But if we allow ourselves this initial distraction, very few of us will take the time to return to ourselves. Helping others is not so helpful when we haven't yet addressed our own nature. How many times have we marveled over therapists who seem crazy, recovery counselors with unacknowledged drug or gambling problems, and self-help gurus who need to take the time to help themselves?

My very serious socialist friend Mark worries that this is a kind of self-coddling. Isn't it just so bourgeois? He's afraid we will spend all our time creating our resonant environments and forget about healing the world. But there is no possibility of this actually happening. Living in an environment that even partially supports your nature is in itself an act of healing the world, albeit a small part of it. Furthermore, once you feel fully supported in who you are, you can't help but bring your gifts out for the world to use. When you express your nature, you influence people positively. There's no way this can't happen; it happens without your consent. So finding your resonant environment is really the primary act of compassion for yourself and for the rest of the world. Besides, by the time you get to the work in chapter 6, you'll wish all you had to do was create a resonant environment for yourself.

This kind of environment sounds great, but how do we get there? Maybe a better question is, Why aren't we there right now? The problem is that when we shine, our light illuminates not only the rest of the world but also ourselves. As we express more of ourselves, we see the truth of who we are — the beautiful parts and the not-so-pretty ones.

Finding your resonant environment can be dangerous — you will get more insight into yourself than you may have ever wanted. It can be a lot easier to trip along, allowing your light to be partially blocked, so that you don't have to see the parts that aren't so nice. It's like not wanting to lose weight because then your hair will look worse. The only way to get around our fear of seeing ourselves is to start by seeing ourselves. We need to begin to tell the truth to ourselves, then to others, about what supports us and what drains us, what really feels right, halfway right, or just plain wrong.

My colleague Susan has noticeable facial hair. I asked her about it once, since we'd become good enough friends to talk about things openly. She told me that she considered her moustache to be an excellent filter — she'd meet men, and if they were put off by it, they weren't right for her. Using her moustache-filter, she found an unusually openhearted, kind, and generous partner.

Truth is a powerful filter. If we allow ourselves to see and accept what is true for us, this truth acts on the world almost of its own accord. It filters out what doesn't work, not by any painful process, but by drawing distinctions. The men who weren't interested in Susan were no doubt relieved to find she wasn't interested in them. By simply letting the truth speak for itself, we can peacefully create the resonance we seek.

Telling the truth not only filters your environment down to what resonates with you, it also magnifies your source. It helps you realize the power that comes from expressing your nature. If we claim the power to be who we are, other people easily see and respect that power. I had a mentor who would rub her belly when she thought of a good experiment. She'd say, "Ooh . . . that sounds yummy!" Of course, this is pretty strange for a scientist. But because she felt comfortable expressing herself, everyone respected her. She oozed personal power from her very source.

TRUTH REACTIONS

I have a friend who returned from a trip to Boston, glowing with exciting stories. She had fallen in love with her thighs, met a wonderful woman, and slept in satin sheets. One of her stories was about an experience she had sitting beneath a tree and thinking about her life. When she found a deep truth, she knew it was right because her whole body tingled; she felt like she was a bell that had just been struck by truth. I had never heard such an excellent depiction of the "ring" of truth.

This story stuck with me, and I began to experiment with truth in myself. I found that when I say out loud something that is crucial to my soul, the hair on the back of my neck stands on end. Other people experience tingling, get goose bumps, or feel "fluttery." It turns out that these physical reactions to truth are very common.

So if you are wondering how you will create your resonant environment when you are not even sure what is really true for you, let yourself discover how truth feels to you. Put your hand on your heart, stand up, and say out loud something you know is true but is sort of scary anyway, such as, "I am afraid I am not loved" (if this is true for you). Then pay attention to your whole body. What do you feel? Now try saying something not true, such as, "I am not loved." It's not the same, is it?

Somewhere you know what is true, even when your mind is confused. When you go to a seminar, read a book, or go to a service, listen for truth. When you go to work, talk to your friends, or spend time at home, listen for truth. If you wonder how you really feel about something, say out loud how you think you feel. Once you experience your truth reaction, the rest of your work is to tell that truth to yourself and others.

Telling the truth creates a world in which you have to keep expressing your nature. If you practice radical truth telling, you find that friends, family, and partners know how you really are. If you start to block your nature, they will notice and say something. Telling the truth is an experiment that supports your nature and forces you into further truth telling. It's a scary shift — hard to get out of once you've done it. But it's the best way to help your source return to its natural brilliance.

The Truth Experiment asks you to consider telling the radical truth, the truth at the root of your feelings. This experiment does not ask you to tell the deep-down truths that hurt people's feelings or damage relationships. It asks you to tell the even deeper-down truths that really alter the way you live in the world. That's why it's an experiment: No one knows how your world will change when you do it. At the same time there is no doubt that what happens will change your world.

THE TRUTH EXPERIMENT

GOAL: *To create an environment in which
your nature is supported and magnified*

STEP ONE: *Notice when you do not feel like yourself.*
Throughout your day, pay attention to any interaction or experience that does not support your nature.
EXAMPLE: Let's say you're aware that you don't

feel like yourself whenever Stephanie walks in the room. The next time you experience this, pay attention to your nervousness.

STEP TWO: *Notice your deeper experience.*

By paying attention to this experience, you may notice something that underlies it. Ask yourself what conflict there may be for you in the situation. You may also notice something that gets in the way of clearing the conflict up right now.

EXAMPLE: By noticing your reaction when Stephanie walks into the room, you discover that you have a little crush on her. What gets in the way of clearing up the experience right now is that Stephanie is your boss and you rightly feel it would be inappropriate to tell her about your crush.

STEP THREE: *Find the deepest truth for you.*

Dig even deeper. What truth underlies this truth? Keep digging until you find your truth reaction. How do you know when you have gotten deep enough? When the truth is about your feelings, when the truth cannot harm someone else, when the truth makes you shudder just to think of telling someone. Once you discover the truth, spend a moment receiving it in your body: Say it out loud and let yourself respond to it. Keep saying it until it becomes a fact, rather than a threat.

EXAMPLE: You dig deeper and discover that you admire people who have a lot of power. By noticing your truth reaction, you realize that you are attracted to these people because you want more power over your life. Saying "I want more power over my life" to yourself makes you cringe. But you go ahead and repeat it to yourself until you are able to accept it as a fact.

STEP FOUR: *Tell the truth.*

Once you are sure you've found the radical truth, tell it to the person whom you are most afraid to tell. As you tell the truth, see if you can remain connected to your nature.

EXAMPLE: Before a meeting you mention to Stephanie, "I realized the other day that I want to experience more power over my life."

STEP FIVE: *Record your results.*

Record how this interaction went for you: How did you feel before, during, and after? Did your energy increase? Did you gain any insights for future truth telling? You may want to keep track of how your environment shifts after working with this experiment for a while.

EXAMPLE: Stephanie smiles in response to your statement and says, "What would you change, if you could?" The two of you get involved in an interesting conversation that eventually leads to changing your work in a vital way.

NATURE

There are churnings inside of you; already you are showing your roots. Feel the way you grow, the way you move. Feel how you turn toward the sun. Feel how you know the soil, your leaves, your strength. This is your nature. Allowing it to be exactly as it is.

What to include in your Unfolding Notebook:

- tools that support your nature
- insights from working with your shame
- results from the Truth Experiment
- discoveries about your resonant environment
- anything else you find on your path

Your work in this chapter is complete when you have discovered how you can

- more completely express who you are right now,
- turn shame into awareness of your needs,
- find the truths that help you shine most brightly,
- create an environment that makes it easy to express your nature.

CHAPTER TWO

PURPOSE

CHAPTER GOAL:

To discover your purpose

After I had dropped out of graduate school and moved back to my Midwest homeland, I spent a lot of time talking with God. One day I felt like I'd gotten a particularly good connection, so I decided it might be the right time to make a few requests. I was confused about my life path, so I asked for clarity: Should I be a scientist or a spiritualist? I was broke and unemployed, so I asked for money. My sister had been diagnosed with a mental illness, so I asked for her to be healed. Once I had listed all my requests, I asked God what I could do in return. The answer came back: Be who you are.

I laughed out loud. I had asked for all these changes, most of which I thought were unattainable, and all I had to do was be who I was? No problem! I was sure I had gotten the better end of the deal.

To celebrate this conversation, I headed over to a church to talk with my new minister friend. As I told him the story, it hit me: God was serious. This was no easy task. God wasn't just saying, "Be who you are." I had to consider the question as well as the answer. It was to my question, "What can I do?" that God had answered, "Be who you are." That is, the full directive was really, "What you can do is to be who you are." I need not just to be who I am but to act in the world from my nature — to *do* who I am. Once I realized this, it occurred to me that maybe God had assigned me a difficult task after all.

The word *purpose* comes from Latin and Old English roots that mean "powerful fire." Purpose is the power that comes from "doing" your nature. You can view fulfilling your purpose as a three-step process: discovering your passion, using your passion to guide your actions, and letting your actions produce their power in the world. All three steps are informed by your nature. It is as if your nature acts as an engine for this wheel of purpose.

> **THE WHEEL OF PURPOSE**
>
> 1. Use your nature to find your passion.
> 2. Use your nature to translate your passion into action.
> 3. Use your nature to discover the power produced by your actions.

MYTHS ABOUT PURPOSE

Ben began many of his phone conversations with, "I've got it! I know why I'm here!" He'd call me to announce his newfound purpose in life. It would always be very compelling — a compassionate, healing, remarkable purpose. I wished him the best, at the same time knowing that a few months later he'd be depressed because it hadn't worked out. That is, until his new, Real Purpose crept up on him. Then the cycle would begin again.

Many of us buy into several myths that end up confusing us rather than clarifying anything about our purpose. The most common myth is that fulfilling your purpose means doing something remarkable and different from anything you've done before. But the truth is that fulfilling your purpose is very simple (if not necessarily easy). You do not need to do anything special, if *special* means "different from who you are." To fulfill your purpose you must do something that should be very ordinary: using your nature to translate passion into action into power.

The second myth, that your purpose has to have a particular quality (useful, peaceful, loving, creative, charitable) to be worthwhile, also comes from not understanding the simplicity of purpose. Your purpose does not have to be anything in particular, and, in fact, it can't be anything other than what it is. At the same time, acting from your nature will never lead to an unimportant, unkind, or useless outcome.

The final myth is that your purpose justifies your existence. Your purpose is not why you are here; your purpose is what you can choose to do while you are here. Not that it doesn't feel good to fulfill your purpose; it's just that you don't have to do it to justify your existence. You don't have to eat chocolate to prove that eating is worthwhile. We are here to live our lives, and if you choose to fulfill your purpose, you will feel fulfilled.

> **PURPOSE MYTHS**
>
> - To fulfill my purpose I have to do something out of the ordinary.
> - My purpose has to be _____ (fill in the blank).
> - My purpose justifies my existence.

Discovering Passion

Don, one of my coaching clients, really loved his carpentry hobby. If there was any way he could sneak this hobby into his work as a sound engineer, he would. If he could use it in his volunteer work, he would do that too. In one conversation I mistakenly told him how great I thought it was that he loved to use his creativity in such a practical way. He was taken aback — he told me that wasn't what motivated him at all. What he really loved about doing carpentry was feeling the wood beneath his hands.

I couldn't relate. I was too busy thinking about what I

might enjoy if I were a carpenter to understand his passion. But I finally understood that for Don, sensuality is where his passion lives. He also loved to paint on silk, swim in heated pools, and brush horses — anything that felt good to his body. When Don is feeling his way through his life, he is at home with himself, living from the source of his nature.

Notice how engaging your sensuality is not, on the surface, the most earthshaking passion. It's not, for instance, feeding the poor, healing the sick, or mediating governmental conflict. When we are discovering our passion, we've got to avoid the temptation to buy into the first myth — the myth that defines for us what our purpose should be. If you can't immediately see how your passion will transform the world, that's perfect. Passion is about what you love, not what you'll do with that love.

THE PASSION PRACTICE

GOAL: *To discover your passion*

STEP ONE: *Remember your nature.*
    Let yourself relax. Make yourself at home in your nature, using the Yes Practice or another practice to let yourself be who you are right now.

STEP TWO: *Name the work you love.*
    What is one thing you've done — job, hobby, sport, or game — that makes you feel in love with life? Is there more than one thing? Write down everything you can think of that has made you feel like yourself. Remember not to force these toward the Mother Teresa end of the spectrum. Watching football games should go on this list if when you watch them you feel at home in your source.

STEP THREE: *Change the work.*
    Read through the list of things you love. Take each in turn, and imagine that it is changed slightly.

Remove elements of it, piece by piece, until it becomes something you don't think you'd love anymore. For example, Don could remove the element of making something if he could keep the feel of the wood. But if he had to do carpentry at a distance, by managing a carpentry company, he'd hate it.

STEP FOUR: *Unite your passions.*

Write down next to each item on your list what you couldn't remove from it without losing your love for it. These are your passions. Look through the list of passions and ask yourself what they have in common. Try out several ideas to see how they feel to you. Once you find a description of your more global passion, write it down.

STEP FIVE: *See if your passion feels right.*

Spend a few minutes right now meditating on what you think your global passion might be. Notice how you feel as you are doing it. Do you feel a bit off center? Then go back to Step Two and recheck your work by making sure it all feels true. On the other hand, if you feel at home in yourself and energized for action, then you have found your passion.

ANGER: A SHADOW TOOL

Jesus is quoted as saying, "Don't hide your light under a bushel." He's got at least two great points. First, if you hide your light no one can see it. We looked at clearing room for your light in the last chapter. Second, if you hide your light under a bushel, the bushel will catch fire — a perfect illustration of how anger can work. The job of passion is to motivate action. But when passion has been blocked and thwarted from its task, it turns into anger. There are at least two kinds of anger, arising from two kinds of blocks.

Indira lived for a time in a battered-women's shelter. She

had been physically abused by her husband, who told her that
if she sought help he would come after her. This certainly was
a block that prevented her action — a severe and tangible one.
But Indira used her anger to topple the block. She realized that
he couldn't hurt her if he didn't have access to her, so she called
a shelter with twenty-four-hour security in another town and
moved there the next week.

The other kind of anger is more chronic. One of my coaching clients was perpetually angry. She would lash out at anyone
in her path, me included. Whenever we talked, she would tell
me a story about why she was angry. Each story was different
on the surface — someone was incompetent at work, there was
an infantile discussion on public radio, she was overlooked for
a promotion. But in fact, the story was always the same. Her
story was that she wasn't really allowed to act in the world.
Someone or something always prevented her from fulfilling
her purpose. When I terminated our coaching sessions and
referred her to a therapist, I became the block for her. The next
day, I'm sure she found yet another.

Indira's anger built up until it could overtake the block,
then her anger pushed it over. This kind of anger is *motivational anger* — it drives us to change our environment. Anger
used this way clears out whatever blocks our passion. The
chronic kind of anger builds and builds without ever overtaking
the block. We stay angry and sometimes have a difficult time
tracing the source of the anger. This second kind of anger, like
my client's, is *protective anger*. The difference between these
types of anger is that in the first case we use the block as a
springboard, and in the second case we use the block as a cover.

Because there are at least two kinds of anger, there are at
least two ways to use it. We can use motivational anger to over-
come blocks, and we can use protective anger to discover why
the blocks are there in the first place. The problem is you can't
always tell the difference between these two kinds of anger. The
only way to move forward is to treat them both the same until

they start to behave differently. By their differences you'll know how to use them.

Here's an example: Your partner leaves the bath mat on the floor, and you get annoyed because you feel like she is taking your natural neatness for granted. You pick up the bath mat and go tell her how you feel. After your initial burst of anger you find it easy to work with her to reach a compromise that suits you both. You are able to move forward without another thought. Once your anger is released and you have used it to change your situation, you can see that this was motivational anger.

Here's another way the same scene could work. Your partner leaves the bath mat on the floor, and you get really angry because you feel like she is taking your natural neatness for granted. You pick up the bath mat and talk with your partner. You are unable to accept any of her explanations, and you can't seem to come to a useful compromise. You are still angry as you leave the conversation. Your inability to reach a compromise with her or to let your anger release itself tells you that this anger is probably protecting something. After doing some work on your own, you discover that you have a very deep concern that if you get close to your partner, you will be taken for granted. You have erected a block that protects you from getting close. You discuss this with your partner, and in your discussions you agree to attend couples' therapy, and when you do you feel your block (and your anger) begin to dissolve.

THE RAGE RITUAL

GOAL: *To begin overcoming and/or understanding your blocks by releasing the power behind your anger*

What You'll Need:

- fifteen minutes alone in a fairly empty, private space with nothing living in it (plants, animals, or other people), a

place where you won't mind making loud and possibly
embarrassing noises

- a safe and unbreakable tool for your anger — punching
bag, pillow, rage doll
- your Unfolding Notebook

1. Go to your private space, bringing your anger tool(s). In
   this space, you will let your anger move through you.
2. Gather all your anger. Imagine your blocks in front of
   you and feel your anger pushing at these blocks.
3. Even if you don't feel angry, move or dance as hard as
   you can. Scream, yell, announce your anger to the
   world with your body and your voice. If you have the
   urge to hit something, make sure to use your anger
   tool(s), not your bare hands or feet.
4. Keep on moving and making noise as you feel your
   anger rise up within you. If your anger starts to slow
   down or turn into something else, go to Step Five to
   work with motivational anger. If your anger keeps
   coming through you for ten or more minutes, go to
   Step Six to work with protective anger.
5. (Use this step for motivational anger.) Notice exactly
   what your anger has become; this is the power behind
   it. Dance and move with your new feelings. Let yourself
   look back at your blocks and discover whether you have
   any further insights about what they were and why they
   were there. Write these insights in your notebook. Use
   your newfound energy to translate your passion into
   action (which we'll discuss in the next section).
6. (Use this step for protective anger.) Slow down your
   anger voluntarily by slowing your movements and
   quieting your voice. As you do, start to dance and
   move to the story of your blocks. It's okay if you don't
   know this story — just let your body move and show
   you how the story goes. Through your movements,

describe each block to yourself. Where did it come from? How is it useful? What would you need to feel safe without it? Once you have described your blocks with your body, write your insights in your notebook. Ask yourself if there is one practical thing you can do to begin dissolving these blocks. Make a commitment to do this, then move on to the next section.

TURNING PASSION INTO ACTION

There are three guidelines you can use to discover specific, practical actions that naturally flow from who you are. The first guideline is to *start where you are*. That means asking yourself how what you are doing right now reflects your passion. As I write this chapter, I am revisiting my passion and asking myself how my writing fits with it. What does this specific act — working on the Purpose chapter — have to do with my passion? If I convince myself that there is no relationship between my work here and my passion, then eating a whole bag of potato chips is potentially more satisfying and far less difficult. So you can see that if you don't force yourself to find a connection between your actions in this moment and your passion, it becomes fairly easy to distract yourself from an action that truly supports your purpose.

If we start from where we are, the question we need to ask is not whether our actions are in alignment with our passions but exactly how our actions relate to our passions. It is possible that what we are doing has nothing to do with our passions, but it is very unlikely. We want to fulfill our purpose, even when we are unaware of what it is. So most of the time some piece of whatever we do is an outgrowth of our passions.

As you find that piece and let it expand until it becomes all of what you are doing, your actions become more in line with your passion. A bank teller discovers that the only time her passion for justice really inspires her actions is when she analyzes bank statements to find errors. She makes it known to her co-workers and supervisor that this is what she loves, and soon she is in charge of error tracking for all personal accounts. An executive makes it clear to everyone in his work group that he loves to facilitate meetings. Within months he manages so many meetings that he starts a successful business as a professional mediator.

The second guideline is to *plan for the short term*. Denise went to school to become an occupational therapist. When she graduated, she spent a lot of time trying to specify her new goal. Was it to start an employee-run gardening store for stroke victims? Or was it to get a grant to build a nonprofit clinic? But Denise needed to back up. It's very difficult

GUIDELINES FOR TRANSLATING
PASSION INTO ACTION

- Start where you are.
- Plan for the short term.
- Respect your nature.

to decide whether a particular action is a direct translation of your passion when the action will take more than a year to complete. We are better off keeping the long-term goals as possibilities and instead spending our time working on what flows from us right now.

Denise was already working as a part-time gardener. When she looked into how her passion came out as she worked, she realized that her passion for environmental activism really motivated the way she worked. She only used organic fertilizers and locally grown plants. She expanded the activist part of her gardening by discussing with her customers why she made these choices.

As Denise expanded her work in this way, she started to notice that her short-term actions were things like "meet people who know how activism works, learn about the environmental impact of human activity, check a book out from the library about how to start nonprofit activism groups." Her short-term actions, each of which naturally flowed from who she was, eventually moved her toward starting a nonprofit environmental activism group — an outcome that she couldn't have predicted. If you do what comes naturally right now, your long-term plans take shape as you do. In a sense, this is the lazy (or efficient) person's way of getting things done in the world.

The third guideline is to *respect your nature*. Your actions need to make you feel like yourself. If you think of your nature as the engine that turns your wheel of purpose, then it's clear that you can't get anywhere by pushing against the engine. You have to move with its force, not against it.

My neighbor Dean had discovered that his passion was doing art. By following the first guideline, he knew that the way his technical writing job served his passion was that he was able to make the graphic designs that went along with the manuals he produced. By following the second guideline, he let this piece expand slowly, taking small and natural steps like having a lunch conversation with his boss about how much he liked graphic design, working on a small website that showcased his graphics, and taking a night course in advanced drawing techniques.

But as he took this evening course, something didn't feel quite right. So Dean spent some time observing how he felt when he was in the class. He discovered that he felt lethargic and not really himself for three weeks in a row as soon as he walked into the classroom. Unlike in most of the other art-related situations in his life, here he wasn't expressing his nature. The fourth week of class, as he checked in again, he discovered why. His next step was not to take an art class, but to teach an art class. Though he was scared when he thought of teaching, he also felt excited. The next day, he called up the community center down the block and scheduled himself as the watercolor teacher for the summer session. By respecting his own nature, Dean brought his actions where they needed to be.

THE POWER OF PURPOSE

Acting from our true selves sends shock waves into the rest of the world. We can see our own power, sometimes for the first time, and it is exciting and electrifying. It is also intimidating, shocking, and frightening, but we'll get to that later. An initial, joyful burst of energy comes from consciously doing even a single action that flows from your passion. As that action expands you start to notice even your smallest movements having a major impact on the world. This is the power of fulfilling your purpose.

I spent a year and a half working in a gray cubicle at a conservative Midwestern pharmaceutical company. Six feet tall, no makeup, and fairly outspoken, I stuck out a bit. But I still tried to pretend that I was part of the crew. Lunchtime conversations, which invariably included racist and homophobic jokes, were especially painful. But I said nothing.

After about three months of this, I couldn't stand it anymore. My boss was telling another employee in our group how strange she thought bisexuals were — that they were the sickest of all the perverts. This did not just stir my passion for creating understanding in the world; it hit me on a personal level, because I am bisexual. My passion brought me to action, and I came out of the closet. My boss started crying.

I got scared. I wore "what-ifs" as if they were hair shirts. What if I get fired for this? Or worse, what if I'm no longer welcome in the group but they feel like they can't fire me? I had seen my power — and it was big. Like many of us, I certainly wasn't used to seeing myself fulfilling my purpose, making a difference. And, like many of us, the sight was enough to temporarily scare me into inaction.

The terrifying thing about power is that it is so, well, powerful. It really moves things. Really Moves Things. It's as if we're on one end of a lever, and we put maybe a pinky's worth of who we are out there on the lever. And the other side, the long side of the lever, lifts a house or jacks up a car. And it keeps on like this. The more genuine our actions, the less effort we need to produce more power. The only way to prevent this kind of exponential power increase from scaring you into inaction is to let the power return to its source. You need to recharge yourself with this energy, otherwise you drain your source and make it impossible to continue fulfilling your purpose.

When I learned how to welcome my own power, it was as if our group had experienced a minirevolution. My boss and I went out to lunch and negotiated a truce, then we actually became friends. I started bringing my books on spirituality and community to line the drab shelves of my cubicle, and people came by to borrow them as if I was the local librarian. Another employee in our group came out of the closet and was accepted without comment. And our lunchtime jokes began to be centered on our personal idiosyncrasies, not on our sexuality or ethnicity.

THE POWER EXPERIMENT

GOAL: *To recharge yourself with the power of your purpose*

STEP ONE: *Do the purpose process.*

Meditate on your passion, then do a small action that flows from it. Allow yourself to experience the power of that action. While you are experiencing this power, close your eyes and imagine power pouring into you, starting at one point in your body and moving all over. Then let it in at another place, and another. Actively receive your power, letting it into every part of you. Give your feelings time to move through you, change, grow, and recede. Do this for at least five minutes.

STEP TWO: *Let the power speak.*

Listen to what the power has to say. What is it telling you about what happens when you are yourself?

What name does it give to itself? Let that phrase, image, or name sink in, and check whether it seems true.

EXAMPLE: I let the power come in and I feel energized, bubbly, and light. It sounds strange, but my power is telling me that it is about "showing off the mysteries of God." Is this right? It feels true, but "showing off God" seems more right.

STEP THREE: *Hit the road.*

Go back to fulfilling your purpose out in the world. The next time you feel that your purpose is not flowing well, do this experiment again. Extend the amount of time you spend receiving your power by five more minutes.

Receiving the power of your purpose completes one turn of the wheel. So what do you do once you've already fulfilled your purpose? You turn the wheel again. Every turn of the wheel brings new elements of passion forward; every turn gives us new actions, bringing new power with them. Even though we each have a unique nature that energizes our distinct passions, actions, and power, all of us have the same purpose: to keep the wheel turning.

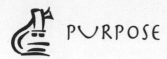 # PURPOSE

A new shoot reaches deep inside, carrying nutrients up its tendrils. It has created an intricate lattice of tunnels, weaving in and out of the tubules that carry water. These tunnels are its own beautiful work, and it is pleased with its efforts. It has used its own nature to further its purpose.

What to include in your Unfolding Notebook:

- tools that help you focus on your purpose
- ways you have used anger to block your action
- specific actions that are driven by your passion
- results from the Power Experiment
- anything else you find on your path

You know you have completed the work in this chapter if you have discovered how to

- find your passion,
- use anger to release your passion,
- translate your passion into action, and
- receive the power of your purpose.

DISCOVERY SOUL MAP: THE WHEEL

GOAL: *To create a tangible reminder of your purpose*

STEP ONE: *Define the circle.*
Label the center of a circle as "Nature/Source," with "Passions," "Actions," and "Power" written on the circle itself.

STEP TWO: *Gather reminders of your nature.*
Find images, words, songs, or anything else that reminds you what you need to support your nature. You might want to include a list of people in your resonant environment. Place (glue, draw, write) these in the center of the circle.

STEP THREE: *Gather reminders of your passion.*
Place anything that reminds you of your passion next to where you've written "Passion" on the circle. You may want to cut out words from magazines or calendars, or draw your own images that describe your passion.

STEP FOUR: *Gather reminders of action.*
Next to the "Actions" label, make a partial list of some actions that you've already done that followed from expressing your nature. You may also want to include images of these actions or quotes that relate to them. List at least three strengths that you needed to complete these actions.

STEP FIVE: *Gather reminders of power.*
Place anything that reminds you of the power of your purpose next to the "Power" label. Again, images can be useful to help celebrate the energy you create when you fulfill your purpose. Draw an arrow connecting your power with your nature. Around this arrow, write words or create images that remind you of returning your power to your source.

STEP SIX: *Define your purpose.*

Somewhere on your map, write down your purpose. Here is a template you can use if you like: My purpose is to continually use my nature to translate my passion for _____[your passion] into action, and to let these actions create _____[your power] in myself and the rest of the world.

EXAMPLE: My woodworking client Don's purpose is to continually use his nature to translate his passion for sensuality into action, and to let these actions create beauty in himself and the rest of the world.

MAY YOUR WHEEL TURN IN BEAUTY AND WISDOM.

PART TWO
MASTER

CHAPTER THREE

FAITH

CHAPTER GOAL:

To develop your partnership with God

When I ended my five-year sabbatical from science, I felt desperate to return to school and study sound perception. But I decided I couldn't. I had applied to several different graduate programs for three years in a row and been rejected. It was already the end of August, and the deadlines for applications had passed. Besides, I didn't want to leave our new house in Evanston to go to some far-off university, and I hadn't paid off my previous debts. I lay in bed one morning and talked with God about all the reasons I couldn't have what I wanted.

Then I started to wonder about what I really wanted instead of focusing on why nothing could work. I realized I wanted to be accepted to a Ph.D. program, even though I had been rejected three times. I wanted to attend a local university rather than one out of state. And I wanted funding so that I wouldn't have to go into debt by becoming a student. Suddenly it became obvious that I would be risking nothing if I just asked for what I wanted.

So I asked for those three things. I was very frightened to ask for them, because I wanted them so much. I feared that if I didn't get them I'd be heartbroken and angry with God. Nevertheless, I took time off work and spent the day at the school down the street, Northwestern University.

By the end of that day, I had been accepted to a Ph.D. program to study sound perception. The deadline had been months ago, but I talked to the registrar and some faculty members and convinced them I was worth it. The registrar laughed and said, "It was only because you were on a mission from God that I even let you in my office!" The faculty got caught up in my excitement and allowed me to give them old letters of reference that I'd saved for nostalgic reasons.

By that evening, I was both thrilled and scared. Everything had gone perfectly. But what if I didn't get funding? I couldn't do anything about that for another three weeks, when the head of the department returned from his trip to Italy. So I waited and kept asking God to make it work. When the department chair returned, he wrote to say I had received funding and a full tuition waiver. When I received the letter, I felt as if God were looking over my shoulder, nodding His head. I know that God and I worked together to make it happen.

CONTINUOUS PARTNERSHIP

In the biblical story of Sodom and Gomorrah, Abraham argues with God about God's plan of destroying the two cities. Abraham talks God into not destroying them if he can find a hundred righteous people in them; then Abraham talks Him down to twenty. Finally, God agrees not to destroy the cities if Abraham can find even one righteous person there. Many of us see this story as a parable about the importance of human life. But it also shows us that we humans are meant to *work together* with God to decide our fate. When we are bold and sure enough to ask God to engage in our lives, we change the course of the world.

But when God looks for a partner, He sometimes finds instead a supplicant, saying, "Please help me get to the game on time; help my cell phone call not break up under this bridge; help me save enough for a new house." Enough of this kind of thing, and eventually even God would get annoyed. After all, we put up a good front about believing that God is a bigger, more amazing being. But our belief comes with strings: If you're bigger and more amazing, why don't you repair my tape deck? When we do this we are choosing to partner with just one part of God — the part that answers prayers.

If we choose to partner with all of God, we find parts of God that we wish were not there. We see that God is not a drug or an instantaneous bliss maker. We discover that our lives are not the sole item on God's agenda. Partnering with God is not about developing an ethereal, airy-fairy relationship with some force of Love. It is about developing an intimate, everyday, every-moment-of-every-day friendship in which you are with God all the time: while doing volunteer work, making a speech, singing in a choir, dancing at your wedding, getting in a fist-fight, eating the third plate of nachos, cursing at pedestrians. All the time.

It's convenient to pray to God — a nice defined time when we can talk about things we want, when we can put in our vote for our lives. But when the prayer is over, that's it — God just goes back to whatever He was doing, and so do we. Or that's how we often see it. But when you enter into a partnership with the Universe, you make a radical change. In a sense, choosing to partner with God is never saying, "Amen." If this scares you, then you might need to update your sense of what God is.

THE LISTENING PRACTICE
GOAL: *To pay attention to your experience of God*

STEP ONE: *State your intention.*

Set a timer or alarm for five minutes. Tell God that you plan to listen for the next five minutes, and you are open to whatever you hear, as long as it is

from God. Commit to accepting any feelings that
come up.

EXAMPLE: If you feel strange planning to listen
to God, say to yourself, "Yes. I feel strange planning
to listen to God," and then move on to Step Two.

STEP TWO: *Listen for God.*

For the next five minutes, be quiet and pay attention to anything you sense during this time. When
you are listening, let yourself just listen without
talking back. God is most likely to speak in a quiet
voice, or not through a voice at all. You may just
have a sense of love surrounding you, or feel an
urge to do something specific. Forgive yourself
whenever you notice yourself drift off, then return
to listening for God.

STEP THREE: *Get a sense of God.*

After you are done listening, write in your
Unfolding Notebook what you "heard." Also
include your sense of what God was like. Did
you see God as a giant forest elf? Did you feel God
as a gentle force, pulsing through the universe?
Let yourself record exactly what your sense of
God was.

I have a wonderful minister friend who can (and will) talk at
length about her view of God. She says, "God is a force, a holo-
graphic entity." And I say, "God is a mother, constantly birthing
us." She imagines God as a universal pattern, hidden and
revealed in the Great Web. I see God as a dark-haired mother in
white and purple robes, gently nudging us along our paths.

In these conversations we always arrive at the same con-
clusion: We don't know what God is, and we never will. Yet we
know for sure how we feel about God, and this is what matters.
What matters is not the way we define God in our minds but
the way we feel God in our hearts. After all, it is the God of our

hearts whom we will come to know. It is the God of our hearts who will join us in partnership.

THE DANCE OF FAITH AND FEAR

Ellen, a talented psychotherapist, told me about a healing she experienced. She was writing in her journal while she awaited knee surgery when she heard a commanding voice. It told her that her knees would be healed in that moment. She sat there, dumbfounded, not sure what to do. As she sat, her knees were healed. Ellen cancelled her surgery, hopped on her bike, and rode around town. Inspiring!

But here's what happened the next day, and the next: Ellen refused to write in her journal, afraid that doing so would somehow evoke this powerful voice. She was terrified by the power of her experience. When I asked her whether she thought she was schizophrenic, she said she didn't think so. She'd actually checked with her shrink. When I asked her if she thought it was God who spoke to her and healed her, she said yes. So then the experience must have reassured her that God

REASONS TO BE SCARED IF YOU FIND PROOF OF GOD . . .

- You could be going crazy.
- If it turns out that God really doesn't exist, you'll feel abandoned.
- This may be the last time you'll ever hear from God.

REASONS TO BE SCARED IF YOU DON'T LET YOURSELF FIND PROOF OF GOD . . .

- You might go crazy and not have God for support.
- If it turns out that God really exists, you'll miss out on partnership.
- You may not hear from God even once.

exists, right? "No!" she answered. She felt scared and didn't know why.

Ellen's story is a very dramatic version of what I call the "dance of faith and fear." Here's how it happens. First we start with faith: We believe God exists and want to be sure of God. At first, our desire to know God gets us motivated. Ellen's faith is what made her able to hear the voice and receive her healing. But when she had proof that God exists, Ellen entered fear. To avoid this fear, she returned to not being sure of God; she returned to faith.

The first step to true partnership with God is to leave faith behind. This may sound paradoxical, but faith is really reserved for things we are not sure of. We don't have faith in our shoes. But we think we need faith in God. In a sense it's true — we do need faith when we are unsure. We need our desire to know God to get us moving toward knowledge. But once we are sure of God, we have to let go of faith. After all, how many relationships flourish when one partner is stuck wondering whether the other one even exists?

In the faith-fear dance, as soon as we get proof of God's existence, we question our own side of the relationship. We may admit that God exists, but what if we're not good enough (smart enough, powerful enough, strong enough, beautiful enough) for God? What if we are a disappointment to God? Our fear drives us back into faith, away from knowledge.

One way to stop swinging between faith and fear is to decide that God doesn't exist outside of us. Maybe if we decide that we *are* God, we won't feel so small and fearful. This way, we don't even get into faith, and we can avoid having any fear at all — or so we think. Actually, this method leads to even stronger fear, since we feel so alone.

Another strategy is to decide that God has no relationship with us. Maybe then we will not have to worry about ourselves in relationship with God. God is just out there, grooving along without us. The problem with this strategy is that we need a relationship with God in order to be sure of Her. In practice, this method keeps us forever stuck in faith.

Both solutions avoid a frightening truth: God exists, and we are worthy of working with God. We secretly know this. Yet somehow it's easy to get comfortable in the faith-fear dance. When we are in this dance, we don't have to begin working with Spirit. We can wonder whether God exists, whether we're good enough for God, or both. We can do this our whole lives. But if we choose to master our unfolding, we've got to stop. We need to become sure of our partnership with Spirit.

FEAR: A SHADOW TOOL

Fear is a wonderful tool. It comes up just before we move through something big. It inspires us to know we are doing something holy, sacred, profound. Fear is like a flashing neon arrow pointing at a turn in our path: "Pay attention now! This is important! You are about to change!"

Even though fear can be a helpmate, it can also feel debilitating. It seems there should be another way to learn about the importance of life changes other than feeling afraid. And there is! At first fear acts as a sign or a pointer. But as we learn how to move, we develop other ways of navigating. To get there, however, we need to know and experience our fears.

Mirror-Fears

Each fear has a mirror-fear, the direct opposite of our conscious fear. While our conscious fear is real, its mirror-fear is often a deeper fear — one we would like to ignore. I worked with a young man who was afraid he would die before he reached age thirty. Because of this fear, he was treading water; he was generally dismissive of his experiences, decisions, and goals. His behavior clearly showed his mirror-fear: He was scared he would *not* die before he reached thirty. If he were really in this life for the long haul, he would have to become more conscious of his path. Becoming conscious of his path was his hidden, deep fear.

I saw another young man who was deeply afraid he was gay. He spent his days wondering if other people saw him as gay, if his fantasies made him gay, or if his way of dressing meant he was secretly gay. His mirror-fear was that he wasn't gay. His deep fear was that if he weren't gay, there wouldn't be anything special about him. So his conscious fear of homosexuality was really a mask for his deep fear that he didn't have anything to offer the world.

Here's another example: A writer in one of my workshops feared that she was evil. She wanted to write, but she was afraid what would come out would be dark and foreboding. When she challenged herself on this, she realized that her mirror-fear was that she is actually a good person. Her deep fear was that if she were to bring her goodness out, she would feel lonely if no one were there to receive it.

These examples bring us back to the two basic fears that drive the faith-fear dance: fear that we have no gifts inside us and fear that there will be no one to see them. Fear that we aren't good enough for God and fear that God doesn't exist. For most of us, these two fears are what have kept us from finding our gifts and bringing them into the world.

> TWO FEARS THAT KEEP US FROM PARTNERING WITH GOD
>
> - We aren't good enough for God.
> - Even if we are, God does not exist.

Using Fear

Faith and fear may seem to be opposites. It seems like the more you fear, the less faith you have, and vice versa. But faith and fear are really both part of the same path. While the job of faith is to get us moving, our fears create the path itself. It is as if we walk on a ridge: We look down one side of the ridge and see "fear of no God" and we look down the other side and see "fear of no good in us." In this way, our fears define where it is safe to walk. Most of us have these fears, so in a large sense, our paths are all the same. But the landscapes of our individual paths are defined by unique manifestations of these two basic fears.

A woman who is afraid she is never going to finish writing her book will experience a different unfolding than someone who is afraid he is going to miss his only chance at love. The unfinished-book woman may walk a path of increased communication with herself, finding her voice, learning about success and completion. The missed-love man may walk a path of finding his center, being comfortable with aloneness, finding love permeating his world. Yet the paths are the same: They are both paths of wisdom, discovery, opening. They are both paths of knowing we are not empty and we do not walk alone. As we find proof of the good in us and of God's eagerness to partner with us, our fears become less powerful. The sides of the ridge gradually become less steep, until the landscape flattens entirely and it is safe to walk anywhere we choose.

This is the way: the middle road, the path we will walk. But it is your unique movements, and the one-of-a-kind gifts you find on the road, that make your path the only one in the universe for you. Your gift to Nature is walking this path, the way only you can walk it. Your gift to yourself is walking this path, the way only you can walk it. By moving through your fears, your path will gently widen, opening for you.

THE FEAR-FACING PRACTICE

GOAL: *To learn how to move through your fears*

STEP ONE: *Name your fear.*
Write your fear in your Unfolding Notebook, describing it specifically and what you think might

happen if what you fear came to pass. Allow yourself to explore your mirror-fears as well, and any
deep fears these mirror-fears might hide.

EXAMPLE: "I fear that if I take this job I'll miss
out on another opportunity. My mirror-fear is that
if I don't take this job, I will get no other offers. My
deep fear is that I am not good enough to do well
at my job."

STEP TWO: *Face your fear.*
Spend a moment imagining your fears are realized.
Write down how you feel.

EXAMPLE: "I imagine I take this job and another
great opportunity comes along. I feel sad and angry.
I imagine my mirror-fear — I don't take this job and
I wait for another offer, but none comes. I feel lonely
and abandoned. I imagine my deep fear of not being
able to perform well in my job. I feel incompetent,
angry, and depressed. I also feel a bit hopeful,
because I actually know I am good at my job."

STEP THREE: *Remember how you stifled your fear.*
Record what you have done in the past to avoid
feeling this fear. Over eaten? Gone out with
friends? Worked too much? Sulked? Surfed the
Internet?

STEP FOUR: *Feel your fear.*
Feel your fear in your entire body. What does that
feel like? What do you intuitively know you need to
do the next time you have this fear? Record what
you think would lead to the most growth and any
commitment you wish to make to yourself about
the next time you feel this fear.

EXAMPLE: "I feel my fear in my belly. It itches!
The next time I feel this fear I will let myself really
experience it. I commit to being with this fear until
I move through it and no longer need it."

ASKING

When we ask God for something, we are saying that God exists and that we are worthy of working with God. It forces us to face both of our fears — that God doesn't exist and we are not worthy of God's partnership. So of course, asking can be a frightening thing to do. We know that if we receive something we asked for, we'll be delighted. But if we don't, we imagine it might prove we didn't deserve it or that God doesn't exist. To avoid feeling these fears, it's easy to arrange a "preemptive strike." The most common one is not to ask for something with our whole selves.

If you ask for what you want with your whole self, you are not holding a piece of yourself back so that you may later say, "I didn't really want it anyway." When you ask with your whole self, you are admitting that every part of you wants what you are asking for, and you may even be hurt and angry if you don't get it.

> **PREEMPTIVE STRIKE**
>
> Using your fear of disappointment to prevent you from admitting what you want and asking for it with your whole self.

When I was a personal coach, I met a group of other coaches in the Chicago area. Denene, one of the most impressive, told me about her plan to get to a conference she wanted to attend. She couldn't afford the plane fare, so she was going to call the president of United Airlines and ask for a round-trip ticket at a deep discount. I couldn't believe it. I was scared for her — I told her that she should be prepared to be laughed at or to not even reach the president at all. To my surprise, Denene laughed at me. I felt sorry for her and hoped for the best.

She called me back the next day and told me what had happened. She had reached the president after all. And he had given her the ticket. Round-trip. And he had asked her to provide his employees with some coaching on how to put themselves on the line as powerfully as she had. Meanwhile, I had been trying to get Denene to do a preemptive strike! Luckily, she had asked with her whole self and not listened to my well-meaning (but wrongheaded) advice.

Asking, like faith, is an in-between state. We want something that we don't have. So we use the bridge of asking. The challenge is being able to ask with our whole selves, then moving to the other side of the bridge and see whether we receive what we've asked for.

THE ASKING EXPERIMENT

GOAL: *To experience how the Universe can partner with you*

STEP ONE: *Define your requests.*
Make ten requests of God, with deadlines. Write these down and date them. Dare yourself to ask for things that you feel are next to impossible — a healing, a call from a long-lost relative, a kiss from a stranger, understanding a difficult problem.

STEP TWO: *Investigate your requests.*
Stay open to what you really want. Spend some time opening up your desire. For example, if you think you want to win the lottery, explore whether money or success is your true desire. But be true to your desire: Don't ask for a chance to play an instrument at a local bar when what you really want is to play bass with the Butt-Kickers at the Double Door. Instead, ask to play bass with the Butt-Kickers at the Double Door. Notice if you close yourself off to something because you fear you won't get it — a preemptive strike. If you find yourself doing this, experiment with the Fear-Facing Practice or another practice that allows you to move through your fear.

STEP THREE: *Ask with your whole self.*
Talk, pray, meditate on what you've asked for. As
you ask, concentrate on the God that lives in your
heart, not your concept of what God should be.
Notice if you feel at home in your nature as you
ask. If you don't, adjust what you ask for or how
you ask until you do.

STEP FOUR: *Record the results.*
Write down whether you received what you asked
for. If you didn't, write that down and keep making
your other requests. Record how you feel about
receiving or not receiving what you've asked for. If
you feel mad at God or relieved, excited, afraid,
overjoyed, or confused, write it down. Your feelings are the keys to uncovering how it feels to work
with God.

The Asking Experiment may seem reckless or selfish. After
all, what if you don't get what you've asked for? Then do you
decide that God does not exist or that you are not worthy?
Actually, there is no question that you will receive many of the
things you've asked for. There is also no question that if you've
asked for enough, there will be at least one request that won't
be granted.

Receiving what you ask for is only a nice by-product of this
experiment. The real result is that you will forge the foundation
of your relationship with God. You already have beliefs and
opinions about how God should act. You have feelings about
any slights or surprises Nature slips you, and you are joyful
when you can feel Spirit next to you. What this experiment
really teaches is that you already have a relationship with God.
What makes God more real than having a relationship with
Her? The truth is in your experience: Here you are, working
with God.

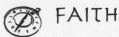 # FAITH

Green shoots stretch and multiply. Roots expand beneath the
soil. A joining of earth and greenness strengthens the plant. It
will grow, turn, and thrust itself through the air with the support
of only its own tools and the love of the earth. It hopes to unfurl
its leaves in time to see the surprise beauty of its flowers.

What to include in your Unfolding Notebook:

- fears and what they have revealed to you
- results from the Asking Experiment
- experiences of you and God meeting head-on
- tools that help you partner with the Universe
- anything else you find on your path

You are done with the work in this chapter if you have
mastered

- an ability to sense God,
- your basic fears about working with the Universe,
- how to ask for things you want, and
- what partnership with God means to you.

CHAPTER FOUR

CHOICE

CHAPTER GOAL:

To choose your soul's path

My high school chemistry professor was very enthusiastic about quantum mechanics. He'd dance around the room with his curly hair bouncing, trying to impress on us smart but hormone-overdosed students that the wave/particle theory of light was truly exciting.

What actually impressed me, besides his hair, was that light didn't have to choose — it got to be made of both waves and particles. I, on the other hand, felt a huge pressure to choose — my future career, my friends, my clothes, even my hypothetical prom dates. At a time in my life when nothing seemed clear, I felt that everything was asked of me. I spent those chemistry classes being very jealous of light.

We begin our lives in the center of a web of choices. Each strand stretching out from us is a potential life path; every path glows with magic. Yet when we are infants, we cannot move on this web. We sit in the center, paralyzed by our lack of life skills. We can't walk or talk, and even our cries come as a surprise to us.

As we grow older, we develop the tools we need to explore

the web. We begin to experiment — taking a few steps down one or two paths, feeling our way. If we are encouraged with loving support, we continue taking steps down each path until we discover what it's like when our steps feel true. Once we've found the feeling of truth in ourselves, we can return to it again and again to test each next step, to continue choosing our way. At the end of our lives, we look back and see what a unique, beautiful web we have woven for our souls.

But this is not the story most of us tell. Instead, we are filled with anxiety, loss, and confusion about our paths. We may find ourselves taking our steps without conviction, wondering if our path is the "right" one. Or we may remain paralyzed in the center of the web, staring in fear at all the possibilities, unable to move at all. We may blast off onto one path, then another, then another, becoming expert seekers without knowing whether any of our steps feel true. However it happens, by the time we are adults most of us have forgotten how to choose our own paths.

God does not have this problem; She has another one. God sits at the center of a universal web, the beauty of every possible path gleaming before Her. But as much as She admires this beauty, God cannot experience a single path. If She did, She would reject all others. God would be in one position in time and space — not everywhere all at once. If God chose a path, She would not be God. Yet even God wants to know what it is like to choose and live in each of Her paths. So God does something miraculous. She gives the gift of choice to us.

God gives us the gift of choice in the hope that we will experience the magic of Her paths. It is our gift to receive or squander. And though none of us are born experts at choice, we can become masters of it. We can remember what it is like to feel truth ringing through us with each sure step. We can recommit to weaving our paths, and know that as we do, we give to both God and ourselves the pleasure of experience. It is only by taking to our souls' paths that we can play with God.

SPLINTERED PATHS

The lonely but much-esteemed Harvard professor kills himself when he finally realizes that life is not about academic success. The cutthroat CEO wakes up in despair to find she has nothing but money. The mathematical genius has no friends; the world-class athlete is too competitive to play on a team. We love these stories and see them played out whenever we can: in books, movies, and television shows. We love them because we know that success in one arena does not foretell success in life as a whole. When there are many paths, moving ahead on one does not predict movement on any other.

The idea that we have many paths — of family, career, spirituality, money, politics, friendship, and more — is a popular one. The belief is that we must balance all paths, so that we move on all of them simultaneously and equally. It is a compelling idea, because we can sense the need to balance all the complicated parts of our lives and ourselves. But the truth is that we have only one path. It is the path of our soul.

The soul's path is torturous. It has millions of curves and changes in direction. But it is the only path that really exists. It is as if we've created these other, splintered paths to run away from the centrality and importance of the soul's path. The soul's path is our "deathbed" path — the one we will look back on and cherish, if we can.

A DEATHBED CHOICE

A "deathbed" choice is a choice that you will be happy you made when you are on your deathbed, even if right now it doesn't make sense. Here's an example: A "deathbed date" is the one you go on even though you have no time and your date lives in another country, yet you still can't get this person out of your mind. (Credit goes to Jeff Shea for inventing this term.)

This is not to say that family, career, money, and so on are not important to our lives. It is that you must collect these

splintered paths back into your soul's path, so that all areas of
your life come together. No more working in one arena while
ignoring other parts of your life. If you follow only one path,
this kind of imbalance is impossible. When you take a step on
your soul's path, everything is taken into account. One step, all
together, on your soul's path beats a million steps, all apart, on
the others. Bringing together these splintered paths is sometimes painful, but once it is done, you will find that real
progress comes easily and feels true.

Recognizing Splintered Paths

My friend Philip enrolled in law school with the intention of
becoming an immigration lawyer. He did well in school and
graduated; no one can deny that he was closer to his goal. But
through those three years of school, something tugged at him.
He was remembering something — it was very foggy, but it
was there. Yet he ignored this tugging and kept to his task.

It took a family crisis to make him realize he had never fully
wanted to go to law school. He had made the decision to go by
dismissing a large part of himself. At the time, it had seemed
the easiest thing to do — to "get on with his life" and begin a
successful career. But once he started to recognize this part of
his life as a splintered path, Philip realized how much easier it
would have been to listen to all of himself and to follow the
truth of his passion — a love for music. He knew he'd have to
continue on his splintered path and feel increasingly numb or
do the hard work of bringing this path back together with the
path of his soul.

We create splintered paths when we want to avoid painful
or difficult steps on our soul's path. We see that if we branch
out and create a new path, we can get closer to our goal without
doing the work our soul asks us to do. We decide that it's okay
to split off a piece of ourselves — say, the career piece — and
make it into a path in its own right.

As we follow this splintered path, we can become seduced by it. For a time we actually move closer to our destination, and we feel vindicated. We think that maybe we're on the right track after all. Our splintered path feels easy, and the real work of our soul seems more and more difficult to do. As we move farther on our splintered paths, we start to forget that there is any other way to move at all. None of this would be a problem, except for the fact that by creating and moving on a splintered path, we lose ourselves.

You know you're on a splintered path when you feel cut off from yourself. You become less and less conscious of where you are and what you are feeling. You do too much and wonder if all your effort is worth it. As a result you may become sick, depressed, or lonely. One way to understand what might have created your splintered paths is to ask yourself questions about what certainly couldn't have created them. You can trick your mind into telling you the truth this way; whatever you've been resisting comes to the surface and screams, "Not me! I didn't do it!" Then you can catch a glimpse of what is really going on.

After my son was born and my husband went back to work, I was in charge of taking care of our new baby all day. I quickly became depressed. I didn't know why. I knew it certainly couldn't be because of the baby. After all, I loved my son and felt nothing but pleasure in being his mom — or so I thought. That was the belief of my splintered "mommy" path. The truth was that I just *wished* I felt nothing but pleasure in being a mother. When I listened to myself, I knew I felt anger about being

SYMPTOMS OF HAVING A SPLINTERED PATH

- You can't stay in touch with your nature.
- You have too much to do and don't enjoy doing it.
- You're not happy much of the time.

completely responsible for another person and grief over losing my old life. Once I identified those feelings, I was on my way back to my soul's path.

Self-Gathering

We leave a little bit of ourselves behind on each of our splintered paths. Pretty soon we are so diluted that we lose touch with God. It is not that God cannot be with us when we are in a million pieces. It's just that when we are so broken apart, it is hard to feel God. God is with each part of us, but unless all those parts can come together, it is very difficult to feel God's presence. God can see all of us, but it is we who need to become more at home with seeing all of ourselves.

Self-gathering means getting comfortable with seeing all of ourselves, with experiencing the feelings that each part holds. When Philip (the former law student) gathered himself together, his path seemed to rise up before him. He was offered a musical internship, he formed a successful band with other local musicians, and (most impressively), he somehow found an inexpensive apartment in a good location in San Francisco.

As you gather yourself, you will not necessarily see your soul's path glowing before you. You may not find a cheap apartment. But you will create an opening — a portal to a new way of living that allows all of you to move together, as one piece. Through this portal lies your soul's path, with all its twists and turns to be discovered and rediscovered as you move with Love.

SELF-GATHERING PRACTICE

GOAL: *To bring all parts of you together so that you can more easily move on your soul's path*

STEP ONE: *Find the parts that were left behind.*
Take a moment to relax and breathe, coming back to your nature. Meditate on your splintered paths; don't worry if you can't name or describe them. Just ask yourself what parts of you have split off

onto these paths. Talk to these parts and tell them of your intention to rejoin them to you.

STEP TWO: *Discover how to join up with each part.*
Here are some questions to ask:

1. (Of the split-off part): What do you feel?
2. (Of the split-off part): What would make you feel okay about joining the rest of me?
3. (Of yourself): Can I give the part what it needs? If the answer is yes, imagine doing so, and see how the split-off part responds.

STEP THREE: *Keep going.*
Let yourself ask these questions of each part that has been left behind on your splintered paths. Know that you may not find all parts that have been lost — that could take your whole life. As you gather yourself, you may identify why you banished each part from you, or you might not. You may explicitly feel the feelings you originally left unfelt, or not. What is important is that you allow yourself to find and remerge with these parts, whatever their meanings. The way you know you have completed this practice (for now) is you will feel relieved, more in touch with your nature, and enlivened.

LOSS: A SHADOW TOOL

My dynamic and eccentric grandmother (she had us call her "Grand-mère") was ninety-four years old when she died. She had walked two miles every day of her adult life until a week before she died of cancer. After four days without food or water, she asked her grown children to come near. Grand-mère told them that she had lived a good life and it was time for her to die, but she needed them to let her go — they had to be willing to mourn her death. It was hard for them, but they agreed; she died the same evening. Grand-mère knew something important about loss.

Loss is the longing for something we've never really had, never had enough of, or feel we can never have again. No matter how long Grand-mère's children held on, they could not have an immortal mother. Grand-mère recognized this and asked them, Do you want to let me go and not have me? Or do you want to not let me go and still not have me? The best thing for her children and for her was the same — to let go of her and mourn what they couldn't have.

As you return to your soul's path, you may find yourself experiencing loss. It may feel like you are depriving yourself of taking so many different roads, since we always lose the paths we do not choose. If you feel loss over the paths you could have taken, remember that you never had those paths in the first place. Knowing that loss is about what we've never had can reduce its power. You don't have it now, so you can either mourn it and move on, or not mourn it and still not have it. We can either let go of the loss or not let go of it. Whichever way we choose does not affect whether we get what we want.

If you avoid experiencing the grief that comes with loss, you may remain stuck on your path. You might not move at all in order to get around feeling your grief. A close friend of mine felt this way: She was stuck because she didn't want to experience the loss of her childhood. She couldn't commit to a career or a partner because that would mean she would be a "grown-up." In a sense, she was afraid to mourn something she couldn't have anyway; even if she were to quit her job every month she would still be an adult. On the other hand, when she chose to mourn and move on, she rediscovered her passion for her career and was able to commit to her relationship. Paradoxically, by mourning the loss of her childhood, she actually felt younger!

GRIEF RITUAL

GOAL: *To mourn your loss*

What You'll Need:

- an object that symbolizes your desire
- a piece of string or rope at least two yards long
  a private place
- your Unfolding Notebook
- fifteen minutes of uninterrupted time

1. Stretch the string between any two points in the room, then place it on the floor. The string represents your grief — the distance between what you want and what you have.

2. At one end of the string, place the object that symbolizes your desire. Stand at the other end of the string.

3. Look around and see where you are — far from what you want and unable to reach what you desire. Spend some time feeling what it is like to long for and yet not have something you desire.

4. Stand near the object symbolizing your desire. Try to feel what it would be like to have what you want and not know any other way of life — having it would be like having oxygen to breathe.

5. Now put yourself in the middle, along the path between the two points. This is the bridge of grief, the place of mourning for what could be. Position your body however you need to express how the grief feels in you.

6. Say out loud, "I don't have _____. And I want _____." Fill in the blanks with what you grieve for. When you feel something shift, gather up each end of the string to meet in the middle,

touching the ends together and crossing the bridge. The shift will fell different for each person. Trust your instincts about when you feel a shift. Record in your Unfolding Notebook how the shift felt and what you now experience.

THE ANATOMY OF CHOICE

Every time we choose something, we need to listen to all parts of ourselves and make sure they are heard and represented. This doesn't mean that we have to do what any particular part dictates — just that each part must be heard. Otherwise, the choice will be at least partly unconscious, and unconscious choices can create more splintered paths. Making a conscious choice requires that you take these four steps: Define the alternatives, understand how you feel about each of them, ask Spirit to guide and support your choice, and make a choice temporarily to see whether it resonates with your nature.

To play with the power of conscious choice, you can expand on the Asking Experiment from the last chapter. In that experiment, you received some things and didn't receive others. Turn the requests that were not fulfilled into choices: "I ask for recognition at work" becomes "I choose to be recognized at work." You can immediately feel the power of the change. Even more power comes when we include God in our choices, as in "I choose to do what I can do and also accept God's help in being recognized at work." A single conscious choice can energize your

---

HOW TO MAKE A CONSCIOUS CHOICE

- Name the alternatives.
- Listen to how you feel about the alternatives.
- Ask the Universe for wisdom and support.
- Make a choice temporarily and find out whether it resonates with your nature.

partnership with God, if you are willing to learn to *share respon-sibility* with God. Sharing responsibility balances two conscious efforts: claiming responsibility for your choice and releasing responsibility for what happens.

Claiming Responsibility

A friend of mine was trying to break an addiction. She went to a recovery program, wondering if it could help her. She walked in the door, and the facilitator said, "Hello! What's your plan for breaking this addiction?" She was silent. He asked her again. She stayed still. What did he mean? Her plan? Why was he asking her questions? She thought it would be the other way around.

She went home and came back the next day, as she had agreed to do. Again he said, "Hello! So what's your plan?" Again she didn't say anything. Same thing the next day. That third evening, however, something shifted. She got up in the middle of the night, excited. "Of course!" she said to herself, "I have the power to create my own plan! I am the one who chooses my life!" The next day she went in and told him her plan.

How do we forget that we choose our lives?

We watch TV or stay on the Internet for hours, and then say we have no time. We borrow money, then complain we are in debt. We become workaholics and then say we are too stressed by our jobs. And we stay in work that does not work for our spirits. All these are strategies for backing off of our responsibility for our lives. They are all ways of making choices without admitting that we are making choices.

Claiming responsibility for our choices reminds God and us that we are committed to and engaged in our soul's work. As we take responsibility for our choices, our unique energy is available to intertwine with God's. Together with Spirit we become powerhouses of creation. We feel closer to God and more able to befriend Him, and God responds with help and resources we didn't know were there for us.

Releasing Responsibility

Even as we are learning to claim responsibility for our choices, we need to remember how to release responsibility for how they are carried out. It seems to work this way: We make a choice, and we take a step. If we choose to work with God, He sends Himself in to help us. Then together with God we walk on our paths. The way God helps is up to Him; what we choose is up to us.

Imagine you are inviting a friend over for lunch. It is your choice to invite him. But it is his choice how to dress, what he talks about, and what he eats. If you are in a true partnership with someone, you don't tell him or her how to behave. And he or she doesn't tell you what to do with your life. Both we and God have our arenas of responsibility. If you work on mastering your arena, you won't have any time to try mastering God's.

There is a story in the Jewish tradition that speaks to this point. A petitioner asked an old rabbi, "If God provides everything, why did God make wheat grow from the ground instead of bread?" The rabbi answered the petitioner: "God provides the wheat, but we must make the bread. In this way God shows us that we are partners in creation."

Sharing Responsibility

We sometimes still find ourselves asking, Whose fault is it if things don't go well? God's or ours? There are two major camps on this issue. First there's the "100-percent responsibility" camp, those who say we are responsible for all events (good and bad) that occur in our lives. On the other hand, there is the "let go and let God" camp. This group believes that everything is God's responsibility and that we are just along for the ride.

The problem with the "100-percent responsibility" philosophy is that it can easily provide an excuse to forgo compassion. After all, poor people chose to be poor, sick people chose to be sick, oppressed people chose to be oppressed. "Let go and let God" is a compelling idea, because so often we fail to release responsibility to God. But it is not empowering; it forfeits our choices — God gets responsibility for everything.

When I was a kid, my parents held encounter groups on the ratty rust-colored rug in our living room. My sister and I would listen from the stairway landing, just out of sight. Our favorite group member was Terry, because she taught us how to cure our stomachaches by having conversations with our bellies. A few years ago, Terry was diagnosed with breast cancer. After her initial struggle with the diagnosis, she chose to create a healing ritual with my help and the help of a mutual friend. During her ritual, Terry greeted the illness and spoke with it, just like she had taught my sister and me. Then we went outdoors to "bury" the cancer in the earth. Terry did not develop her healing ritual as a way to cure the cancer but as a way to cherish what her cancer could teach her. Nonetheless, it has been four years, and Terry is still cancer free.

You can argue, if you're a fan of "100-percent responsibility," that Terry chose her cancer so that she could work out something emotional or spiritual. You can argue, if you're a fan of "let go and let God," that Terry got her cancer because it was God's choice, part of an unknown and unknowable plan.

But you can't argue with her experience. Once she got cancer, Terry chose to move with it, play with it, and see where it took her. She reclaimed her soul's path by activating the power of her choice — she took 100-percent responsibility. And she let God into her path by giving some of her control away — she let go and let God. It doesn't matter whether we chose what has happened to us; what matters is what we choose now. Do we ignore our soul's path, separate from it, and hide our feelings? Or are we present, active, enlivened, and willing to step consciously on our paths, playing openly with the Universe?

THE PATH EXPERIMENT

GOAL: *To discover the choices that will take you into your future*

STEP ONE: *Brainstorm your choices.*

Sit down and relax. Set a timer or watch for two minutes. Get out your Unfolding Notebook and something to write with. For the next two minutes, write down everything that you choose right now. Challenge yourself to get it all down in two minutes. Include everything from changes in your body, job, home, and relationships to things you choose to maintain as they are. When the time is up, stop writing. (Timing this exercise forces you to write quickly and not edit yourself. If you have not written everything you choose down, let yourself have another chunk of time.)

STEP TWO: *Choose your choices.*

Now read your list aloud, as slowly as you need in order to feel your response to each choice, to really feel whether you choose each one. When you are done reading the list, say, "I choose all this." If any one choice is nagging at you, adjust that choice until you are sure it is what you choose.

STEP THREE: *Ask every part to come with you.*

Listen to find out if there are other parts of you that don't agree with your new choices. Ask the Universe for guidance in the choice, and listen for a reply. If a choice now does not seem right, try choosing something else. Once you have found the choices that fit, ask all parts of you to come with you as you walk your path. If all parts of you agree, move on to Step Four. Otherwise, go back to Step Two.

STEP FOUR: *Play with God.*

Tell yourself and the Universe your new choice, out loud if possible. Use the resources you have and any that come to you to support this step on your path. If you find yourself not supporting your choice, there is a part of you that is not being heard. Forgive yourself for not hearing this part, then go back to Step Two.

EXAMPLE: "I thought my new choice was to become more aware of my needs and make them known to others. It worked okay at home, and I enjoyed being with God as I made my new choice. But when people at work have asked me what I needed, I haven't answered honestly. What's up with that? I'd better go back and find out what part of myself I'm ignoring."

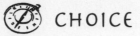 CHOICE

No longer working by design but by its own rules, the stalk climbs its unique and meandering path up the garden wall. Each turn represents trust in the future, a knowledge that is as sure as stone. Tendrils that grasp and hold do not work in fear, but in strength. Faith is lost on this plant; its work is now to choose.

What to include in your Unfolding Notebook:

- insights your loss has given you
- new choices you are making
- results from the Path Experiment
- tools that helped you master choice
- anything else you find on your path

You have completed the work in this chapter if you have mastered how to

- reenter your soul's path,
- use your losses to move you forward on your path,
- take conscious steps on your path, and
- share responsibility with God.

MASTERY SOUL MAP:
PARTNERS ON A PATH

GOAL: *To create a tangible reminder of how it feels to travel your path with Love*

STEP ONE: *Prepare for a journey.*

Imagine that you are about to set off on an adventure. You will walk a long path. You are not sure where it is headed or what you will find. You are not sure what you need to bring with you — you don't know what the weather will be like or if you will stay on the path for weeks, months, or years. You only know that you have chosen to take this journey. First, take the journey (Steps Two to Five) with only yourself; try to ignore God's presence. Then take the journey along with God, actively imagining God is with you on every step. If you like, jot down notes about your journey as you travel.

STEP TWO: *Take to the path.*

First, place a marker in the ground where you begin. This marker will remain here through the entire journey, so you will know you are home when you return. Look at the marker you choose. What is it? Now take the first step. Look at your feet; look at your whole body. What are you wearing? What are you carrying with you?

STEP THREE: *Face your challenges.*

After some traveling, you come across a shape. As you keep walking, it gets bigger. What is it? Soon you are lost. How do you get back on the path? You travel some more — by now you are a seasoned traveler. Yet you find yourself surrounded by danger. How do you move beyond it?

STEP FOUR: *Experience your gifts.*
You look down and find three presents lying along your path, with your name on them. What is your name? You open these gifts. What are they? After some time alone, you approach two people; one is a friend and one is a stranger. Both have a gift for you, and you have a gift for them (these can be material or immaterial gifts.) What do you exchange?

STEP FIVE: *Return home.*
You return to the marker you placed on the path at the beginning of the journey. What does it look like?

In your Unfolding Notebook, quickly complete these sentences:
I can begin my journey when I _____.
I meet challenges best when I _____.
My gifts are _____.
I need God to _____.

STEP SIX: *Create your map.*
When you have completed the journey twice, draw, paint, make a collage, or write about your experiences on each of your journeys.

BLESSINGS ON YOUR PATH!

PART THREE

SHARE

CHAPTER FIVE

CONNECTION

CHAPTER GOAL:

To share your soul's gifts with others

At a recent scientific conference, I presented my findings from two experiments. I gave two talks — or rather, I gave the first, and I shared the second. During the first talk, I felt disconnected from what I was communicating to the audience. I wasn't sure that I really understood the experiment, our interpretation, or why it mattered. The talk lasted for only fifteen minutes, but it felt like a geological epoch. When I was done, the moderator asked if there were any questions. The sea of blank faces and watch glimpsers was overwhelming. Even the moderator, whose entire job was to keep time and ask questions when no one else had any — even he had no questions. I knew what no questions meant. No questions meant I had bored everyone. This was no surprise, I realized afterward, since I had bored even myself. That was the talk I gave.

My talk two days later had a completely different feel. I walked into the room with confidence and love. I had analyzed the results in every possible way. I had mastered and learned to love them. I got up there and told the truth about the experiment; I told on myself for not understanding things and then rearranging my thinking to get a better interpretation of what had happened. I laughed (and the audience laughed with me) about how emotionally close I had become to the findings.

When it came time for questions, there were so many the moderator had to cut them short. Later that day, several people whose work I respected approached me and complimented my talk. The next day, when I was attending a group of talks on a related topic, a very senior and well-respected scientist stopped me as I walked through the room. He said, "That was an excellent talk yesterday." I thanked him and prepared to move on. He stopped me again and smiled. "No. It was a superb, superb talk." *That* was the talk I shared.

THE MATHEMATICS OF SHARING

Sharing is the basis of human connection. When we share something with someone else, we don't share the thing itself, we share the experience of the thing. When I shared my talk with the audience, the audience did not receive the talk. They received an *experience* of the talk. Even when we share material things with others, what we are actually sharing is an experience. When I share a pizza with my friend Dan, though we eat separate slices, the experience of sharing comes from eating parts of the same pizza. Without such shared experience, we would have no way to connect with other people.

On the other hand, when we give something to someone else, we are saying that we do not want it. If we had wanted to continue to have an experience of it, we would have shared it. Instead, we must want to get rid of it entirely. In fact, the recipient should feel a bit slighted — the experience of whatever they are receiving is not something the giver wants to have. Why should the recipient then want it? In my first talk, I was saying to the audience that I didn't want this experiment or these results. They were up for grabs.

The mathematics of sharing are simple. When you share an experience with another person, two people gain the delight of the experience. When you give an experience to another person, you don't have any delight, and often the recipient doesn't either. Sharing continually opens up a circle of delighted people. Giving reduces that number to at most one person. Sharing increases delight, while giving either reduces it or makes it constant.

When we base our relationships on sharing, we form lasting connections with others. I am acquainted with a couple that knows how to use sharing in their relationship quite well. Neither partner is afraid to share her favorite (and less-than-favorite) experiences with the other. Melissa will bring Chris home a favorite chocolate dessert and wait to eat it with her. Chris will carefully open up to Melissa and tell her exactly who she has a crush on at work and why. Then they will share the experience of the feelings that come up for them.

They could also try to make giving the basis for their relationship. In giving, each partner would distance herself from what she gives to the other. Melissa would bring home a favorite chocolate dessert and claim she's not hungry, letting Chris eat it alone. In an offhand, careless way, Chris would tell Melissa that she has a crush on someone at work. Then Chris would defend herself when Melissa attacks, instead of retaining a sense of ownership over what she had said. In sharing, we are brought together — even when what we share is difficult. In giving, we are broken apart — even when what we give is chocolate.

Sharing Your Soul's Gifts

I remember when Sierra, a friend who was always worrying about something or changing her life around for the thousandth time, first showed me her artworks. They were black-and-white photographs, mostly of natural scenes, and they were beautiful. As she described the stories that led her to shoot each photo, she turned from worrywart to genius. This was no small transition.

Sierra lost her anxiety and her confusion, and her work just poured into my eyes.

In contrast to Sierra's pure love for her work, here's how I started to tell people about this book. First I'd say, "Well, it's kind of hoo-hoo, a New Age thing." Then I'd go on to tell them, "I'm not sure I like the title." Finally, I'd finish with, "It's sort of about finding who you are and sharing your gifts with the world. Big topic, I know." And if that rousing summary didn't drive them away, I'd discount the book even more.

I didn't want to actually associate myself with the book, in case someone thought it was stupid. I wanted to separate myself from this book — one of the gifts that is most important to my soul. At the same time, I desperately wanted someone to say, "Wow. Your book sounds totally cool." And of course, no one would. What I was doing was giving away the book, as if I didn't want it myself.

So I chose to do things differently. I looked at why I needed to distance myself from the book and discovered all sorts of anger, fear, and grief from not being fully accepted by my peers. Like many of us, I did not feel well loved in junior high, and I never seemed to get over that. I was hedging my bets with the book — leaving a gap so that I might be accepted even if my book wasn't. One morning I realized that I was repeating my own real, if small, childhood trauma with this book. I wasn't loving the book. I realized that if I didn't love it, no one else could. I couldn't share my gifts unless I loved my work. Once I started telling people about this book I loved, they not so magically started to love it too.

Sierra's story is compelling because we experience it so rarely. My story is more the norm. There is practically an epidemic of people separating themselves from their gifts, hedging their bets in hopes of love, acceptance, or connection. Ironically, we can experience none of these unless we love, accept, and connect with the gifts of our souls.

LOVING YOUR GIFTS PRACTICE

GOAL: *To learn how to love your soul's gifts so that you can share them with others*

STEP ONE: *Appreciate the glow.*

When you fulfill your purpose, your work glows. Whether it's a physical product you've made or some more ethereal service you've done, let yourself see the glow that surrounds your work. Spend a few moments appreciating that glow.

STEP TWO: *Appreciate the mistakes.*

There are also plenty of problems with what you've done; nothing's perfect, right? So let yourself now see some of the mistakes you've made in your work. Spend a few moments appreciating the mistakes you know about and those that you don't. If you can't get to a place where you appreciate your mistakes, move on to the next step.

STEP THREE: *Love your gifts.*

Bring the glow together with the mistakes, and love the entire package. If you don't feel love for the whole thing, see if you can love just one piece. Do you love the way you bring humor into the world? Do you love the color you used to paint the bookshelf? Give a name to the part (or parts) of your work that you can love; these are the gifts of your soul. Then expand that love outward, until it encompasses everything.

JUDGMENT: A SHADOW TOOL

One way to block your love for your soul's gifts is to use judgment to block your love and acceptance of yourself. Judging is deciding that part of someone or something else is unacceptable or unlovable, when in fact it is part of you that you believe is unacceptable or unlovable. When we use judgment to block our love for ourselves, we misuse it. Its true use is to help us become more capable of sharing ourselves. As with all shadow tools, we don't need to remove judgment from our emotional repertoires. We just need to practice using it in the right way.

David is a former colleague of mine from the corporate world. He would sit in our meetings scrunched against a wall, chair tilted back, as if he were trying to evaporate. He rarely contributed anything to the discussion, and if he did, it would be negative. On the other hand, there was Seema.

> ### JUDGMENT
>
> Judgment stems from believing that part of you is unlovable. When we see that part represented in someone else, we judge her or him instead of learning to love and forgive ourselves.

Seema constantly concerned herself with the comfort of others. Several times in a meeting, she would ask David and the others if they were okay, if they needed anything to change.

At lunch one day David confided in me that he never connected with Seema. In fact, she annoyed him. He felt that by being a vocal advocate for the comfort of others, Seema was constantly asking others to meet her need for reassurance. He resented that Seema did not hesitate to ask others to meet this need. David felt like she needed all the attention in a room to be focused on her, all the time. Clearly, this grated on David.

What is the true part of David's experience? The true part is that Seema concerned herself with the comfort of others, and David never connected with her. The rest is judgment. Here's how judgment does its transformational work. First, David needed to notice that he was making a judgment. The tip-off is that he didn't seem to be able to connect with Seema, and this annoyed him. He named the judgment — "I feel like Seema has a big need for reassurance, she feels no hesitation to ask others to meet this need, and she needs all the attention in the room focused on her."

Once he noticed the judgment, he could turn it around and aim it at himself. "I am constantly asking others to meet my need for reassurance. I wish I felt okay about asking others to meet this need — I wish I were as open about my needs as Seema. Furthermore, I'd really like it if all the attention in a room were focused on me, all the time."

When David used his judgment to learn about himself, Seema became a gift to him. David got to see his needs that never got met — the David who never felt like he could be the center of attention, never felt like he could freely ask for what he wanted. David befriended Seema by playing with his own judgment and her concern for comfort. Once when Seema asked if anyone needed anything, David said, "I would be more comfortable if you sat to the left of the door — no, maybe to the right — no, I was right the first time. The left. That's better." Seema got it and laughed. David smiled and finally leaned in to the conference table.

When I lived in San Francisco, I lived down the street from a mother who loved her kids passionately. I used to hear her on my way to lab, praising her children for doing the simplest things — waiting patiently for the school bus or not eating the snacks in their lunch boxes. I thought she was the perfect mother. As I got to know her, I discovered that she had been abused by her mentally ill mom. At sixteen, she ran away from home and never forgave her mother. She never let her mother spend time with her kids. Yet in full daylight one day she slapped her oldest daughter for talking back. Of course she immediately apologized and hugged her daughter, telling me later that she may never forgive herself.

This is not an uncommon story — researchers have long noticed that people who are abused as children are more likely to abuse their children. The part that struck me was her consciousness about not wanting to hurt them, and the fact that this consciousness did not protect her from the act. What did protect her was that she got herself into therapy and worked on forgiving her mother and herself. And though she forgave her mother, she still listened to the wisdom that told her never to leave her children alone with their grandmother.

The reason I bring this story into a discussion of judgment is that I want to make a distinction between wisdom and judgment. It was wisdom that told this mother, as a young woman, to get away from those who abused her. But it was judgment that prevented her from forgiving and loving her mother — and ultimately made it difficult to forgive and love herself.

WISDOM AND JUDGMENT

- Wisdom tells you that you deserve to have your needs met.
- Judgment tells you that you and others are unlovable and undeserving.

Wisdom tells us how to live safely and meet our needs. We need to listen to our wisdom and follow its advice. On the other hand, judgment tells us that the person we are judging is unlovable. This is always wrong. To find the good hidden in our judgments, we need to do some work.

Each person, for the most part, receives equal capacity for gentle, loving, kind acts and for not-so-gentle, hate-filled, mean acts. These are just capacities for actions, not actions themselves. One person may express their capacity for wrongdoing more often or in more severe ways than another person, but it is inaccurate to believe that any single person lacks the capacity to do something wrong.

For instance, when I heard about a murder in our town, I reflexively thought, "There must really be something wrong with that person. I could never do that." I was right — there was something wrong with that person. I was also wrong — I *could* do that. I immediately remembered my son, and how I would not think twice about killing someone who tried to hurt him.

Judgment about another person's actions is a clear sign that we do not accept the roots of their behavior in ourselves. This is dangerous. The roots of every behavior exist in all of us, whether we accept them or not. If we don't accept the roots in others, we cannot accept them in ourselves. And if we don't accept the roots in ourselves, we often end up expressing the behavior. The good in judgment comes when we let it lead us to forgiveness. If we forgive the roots of the behavior in others, we can accept the same roots in ourselves.

THE FORGIVENESS PRACTICE

GOAL: *To turn judgment into appreciation and love for ourselves and others*

STEP ONE: *Name the judgment.*

Set aside some time (about five minutes) to really get clear on your judgment about another person. Also see if there is anything you did to contribute to the situation in which you made the judgment.

EXAMPLE: I think Kathy was unfeeling at the party. She made fun of Michael as soon as I walked in the door with him. Of course, now that I think of it, I poked fun at him first. Still, I wanted her to take the other side and say something about how great he is.

STEP TWO: *Reflect the judgment.*

Now switch positions — make the judgment about yourself. It doesn't have to feel true; just try it out.

EXAMPLE: Well, okay, let's say I was too unfeeling. Maybe not at the party — maybe another time. I certainly have been unfeeling before — when I want approval, for instance, or when I am scared of interacting with someone.

STEP THREE: *Ask for forgiveness from others.*

Ask for forgiveness from the person you judged as well as from anyone else you might have wronged in this situation. As you do, let yourself appreciate and love the truth inside them. They do not need to accept your love or forgive you, but you need to give them the opportunity.

EXAMPLE: I need to ask forgiveness from Kathy for making that judgment against her. She's certainly not an unfeeling person in general, even though she doesn't really resonate with me. Also I need to ask forgiveness from Michael, whom I made fun of at the party and with whom I've been inconsiderate in the past. I feel really lucky to have him.

STEP FOUR: *Ask for forgiveness from yourself.*

Ask yourself to actively forgive what you've done. As you do, let yourself appreciate and love yourself for the truth that is really inside you. Listen for any wisdom that speaks to the situation.

EXAMPLE: I ask for forgiveness from myself for being unfeeling and not very up-front about my true feelings. My wisdom says I don't have to hang out with Kathy if I don't want to. Maybe I'll take a break from her.

RECOGNIZING YOUR GROWTH COMMUNITY

When my grandmother was alive, she was always reminding me to not make assumptions. She came into the DJ booth once when I was doing a show, trying to look cool. Over the ear-splitting tunes, she yelled boisterously, "Hip-hop music reminds me of when I used to play bongos in Paris." Suddenly I didn't feel half as cool any more. Although my grandmother is gone, her memory still influences me.

Then there's Kelly, who always calls at a bad time and wants to get together. I don't really like him but can't ever seem to find the right way to say this. In fact, his nature doesn't resonate with mine at all. But my relationship with him must mean something to me, because I keep being in it. Somehow I say just the right thing to keep him around as a pseudofriend.

We are surrounded by people who keep reappearing in our lives and minds. These people can be living or dead, they can be friends, relatives, or people we've never met. They can be people we respect and love or people we really dislike. They don't need to know or have any special relationship with one another. These people create your growth community.

In the first chapter, you worked on finding the people who resonate with who you are. To be sure, most people in your resonant environment are also in your growth community. But so is that annoying woman at work and the neighbor who never lets you sleep past 6:00 A.M. Unlike with our resonant environments, we don't really choose who is included in our growth communities. That's the bad news. The good news is that creating a growth community is one piece of work you don't have to do, because it gets done for you. Every day people enter and leave your growth community. The key is to identify your growth community and then use it as a tool for your growth.

When we talk about "creating community," finding a partner, or seeking friends, we often say we're looking for people who "match" with us. Instead, what we really want are people who "fit" with us. People who match — those with the same gifts as us — don't really interest us. They don't spend much time, if any, in our growth communities. We tend to ignore them or feel neutral about them. They may resonate with us, but they do not help our growth, because they have gifts that we don't need right now. What helps us grow is to find someone who has the gifts that we need.

> ## MATCHES AND FITS
>
> - Matches are people who are easy for us to be with and carry gifts that we don't need right now.
> - Fits are people who are more difficult for us to be with; they carry gifts that help us grow.

People who "fit" with us — those with gifts that we need for our growth — are the people we have strong feelings about. These are the ones who end up in our growth communities, whether we want them there or not. A fit with someone means there is something to do in your relationship. A fit means there is something to play with, learn from, struggle with, create, or heal. It doesn't mean you share the same sense of humor, like the same movies, and both crave long walks on the beach. Looking for your fits rather than your matches can create radical friendships in which you may not like each other, but you've agreed to work on something together.

A coaching client of mine told me about a member of her growth community who she didn't think should be there. This was a guy who doggedly asked her out, despite what she took to be her continual rejection of him. She felt like she was doing everything possible to be rid of him. But there was clearly some work for them to do, or he wouldn't still be around. Finally, she realized that he presented an opportunity for her to get over her fear of being unloved.

When she examined herself, she realized she had been too subtle in her rejections — making excuses instead of being up-front with him. She was too afraid to reject him outright because she didn't want him not to like her. She invited him for coffee and told him explicitly that she was not interested and would not like to hear from him again. True to her expectations, he didn't like her anymore. He took it hard but got over it quickly, and he no longer showed up in her life. And she was able to look at why being liked was so important to her.

If one person feels they fit with you, but you don't feel that fit, this means you both have work to do. There is a fit in the sense that for now, you two are linked and will be linked until there is agreement to move on, until the work that is needed has been completed. This does not mean that everyone in your growth community requires difficult work from you. It just means that some people in your growth community present very powerful opportunities for growth, while others present less powerful (and usually more pleasurable) ones. You get to choose what work you'd like to do, with the stipulation that the work you ignore will keep showing up.

But let me make one thing clear: You need to consciously surround yourself with the people in your resonant environment. Period. Your growth community will exist whether or not you want it to. You don't need to seek people who challenge you — they will come to you. If someone is cruel to you or demeaning, they are in your growth community. But you can use their gifts without coming near them ever again.

GROWTH COMMUNITIES

Your growth community consists of a group of people (dead and alive) about whom you have strong feelings. For each person in your growth community, you may either

- love them! (like them a lot, admire them, and so on) or
- hate them! (are annoyed by them, don't understand them, and so on).

The purpose of recognizing your growth community is to recognize the others who will share your soul's gifts, and whose gifts you will also share.

If you spend a day consciously identifying the members of your growth community, you'll notice how throughout even one day, your community changes. A new member is added as you meet a truly insipid coworker; another member is taken away when a crush dies down. Over time, each member of your growth community will annoy you or resonate with you. It all depends on whether their gifts lead to difficult insights or easy ones.

TRANSFORMATION: THE FIRST REPAIR

My friend Terry, for whom we held the healing ritual, told me that being a healer means two things. It means doing the act of healing others, which is how we're used to thinking about it. But it also means being a healer in the same way someone might say they are a runner. It means being one who is in the process of healing themselves. Both kinds of healing happen simultaneously. And both kinds of healing expose our soul to the world.

We reveal our soul when we share its gifts. And we see the souls of others when they share theirs. When we show our gifts to the world, we create a beacon so others can find our source. We are saying, "There is a beautiful source here; let my light show you the way." As they see we have a source, their source is tickled — they are reminded that they have one too. These beautiful stars that live within us are made to be seen. In fact, the world can only work when they are all revealed. Showing our truth and seeing the truth in others is the first step in repairing the world.

When I was doing a stint as a spiritually oriented radio talk-show personality, my cohost and I spent the shows interviewing authors, mystics, and psychics. We tried to be as revealing as possible, because we were committed to an honest and forthright show. We wanted to avoid being "out there" as much as we could in that genre. But we were still very safe, behind the glass.

One day our interview subject came into the studio and sat down at a microphone between us. He was a local intuitive who was becoming notorious for his frank insights and his obnoxious, yet somehow contagious, laugh. He took the audience and both of us through a centering process that had us feeling the energy of our source. We both had the feeling that we really loved who we were, yet we were afraid that no one else would love us. We got in an enlightening discussion about this fear and spent the rest of the show feeling fully revealed and alive.

What we discovered through talking with our guest and the audience was that most of us fear that if we let ourselves be seen down to the core, we will be rejected down to the core. But if we don't let people see our source, we won't have to feel so deeply hurt when they reject us. This is exactly the same experience as wanting to separate ourselves from our gifts so that in case they are rejected, we won't be. And it works quite well, in one sense.

If people reject us when we are not sharing our gifts, we don't feel as hurt as we would be if we put ourselves on the line. On the other hand, we won't feel accepted either. We won't have the experience of healing that we need to have. Instead, we'll feel isolated and stifled. We'll feel isolated because we won't be able to receive the healing that comes from others; for that healing to work it needs access to our source. We'll feel stifled because we have a natural drive to share our work, and we cannot fulfill that drive if we won't let ourselves be seen.

The beginnings of repairing the world rest on this modest step, and most of us find it challenging. If sharing our soul's gifts is so important, why should it be so hard? Why should this be the way things are? Because the intensity of the labor draws our attention to the work itself. We become conscious of its importance. As we become practiced at sharing our gifts and seeing the gifts of others, we can more easily see that as we mend one another, we mend the world.

THE OPENING EXPERIMENT

GOAL: *To take the first step in repairing the world*

STEP ONE: *Choose someone to share with.*
   Think of a person in your growth community. That person does not need to be in the room with you, but having him or her with you can help.

STEP TWO: *Share their gifts.*

Imagine receiving all the light she or he wants to share with you — sharing all her or his gifts. Visualize a luxury of light. Remember that you are sharing her soul's gifts and seeing her source — not her external personality. Share the gifts and let them come into you, doing their healing work. What does this new light show you about you? How does it change you?

TIP 1: If you are doing the experiment with someone else, she can start with Step Three as you do this step.

TIP 2: Try this with each of your parents as the light sharers — it's an amazing experience!

STEP THREE: *Share your gifts.*

Once you have received to completion, practice sharing your gifts with this person. If you are doing the experiment with someone else, now she can do Step Two. Pour all the gifts you can give freely and joyfully into this person's lap. Remember as well to let the light remain with you so that you are not giving anything away, just sharing what you have. Allow the light to continually flow through you to this person. How does sharing this light feel to you? How are you changed?

STEP FOUR: *Repeat with everyone.*

Record in your Unfolding Notebook the gifts this person shared with you and the gifts you shared with him or her. Try this one every day. Let yourself do this experiment with everyone in your growth community, as many times as you like.

⟨👁⟩ CONNECTION

In preparation for harvest, the plant uses the sun to seal off its broken stems. It nourishes its roots, storing rain for the dry fall. It keeps starch in its fruits, strong and ripe, ready to drop. Into the soil it sends firm rootlets, holding hands with the earth.

What to include in your Unfolding Notebook:

- tools that help you love your gifts
- what your judgments have shown you
- results from the Opening Experiment
- any experiences of transformation within your growth community
- whatever else you find on your path

If you finished the work in this section, you will have begun to share

- the gifts of forgiveness,
- your soul's gifts with the world,
- the gifts of others with your soul, and
- conscious and transformational relationships.

CHAPTER SIX

CREATION

CHAPTER GOAL:

To create healing in
the world

W hen I was in graduate
school for the first time, I somehow convinced my thesis advisor
to send me to a neuroscience conference in Schiermon-nikoog.
Schiermon-nikoog ("island of the monk's eye" in Dutch) is a
small, fog-blanketed island in the Netherlands. It is a perfect
place to think heady thoughts about how the brain might work.

During one of the breaks, I rented a bike for two dollars and
rode around the island. As I rode, I noticed a field of grass gone
to seed, and above it I saw a circle of gulls. The circle really
impressed me. Though it's a common sight for coast dwellers,
this circling was quite beautiful to my Midwestern eyes. As I off-
roaded toward the field, I could see the gulls more and more
clearly. When I was close enough to the seagulls' circle, I
hopped off my bike to lie in the grass and stare up at the birds.
I could see the path that each bird in the circle was creating, and
a chill coursed through me when I realized that not one bird was
flying in a circle.

One bird did an arc about a quarter of the length around
the circle, while another flew up and down, defining the edge of

the circle. Another gull flew about a half of the circle then returned by retracing its path. But not a single seagull flew the entire circle, even though as a whole their circle was so clear I could trace it in the sky. The experience shook me. I heard myself whisper, "I thought I had to do the whole circle," and I felt tears pressing against my eyes.

Years later, a friend of mine studying theology casually mentioned to me that one thing she thought was cool about Islam is the idea that we are all holding part of a universal wheel. No one has the whole wheel, but we each have a part. Our job is to turn our part. Of course we wonder about the plan for the universe and how it will all work out when it all seems so weird and painful and crazy, since we can only see our part of it. But no matter what, our job is to keep turning our part of the wheel.

GOAL COMMUNITIES

As I thought more about this idea, I noticed that the scientific community (at its best) works like the gulls or the Islamic wheel. Each of us must discover our work and master our paths. But then we have to look past our own experiments to see what others have done and where our discoveries fit. By sharing our results with others, we bring a piece to the puzzle. But then by receiving feedback and ideas for possible collaborations, we can learn more than we could all alone. The community of scientists swims in this pool of history, trust, and collaboration, because otherwise we could not make any progress at all.

Of course, some scientists choose not to swim in this pool. And often they don't benefit from that choice. For instance, scientists who don't want their work to be reviewed by their peers won't get published in respected journals. Or scientists who don't refer to supporting evidence and take all the credit for themselves may not receive funding for their research. Similar misfortunes strike people who want to cut themselves off from their neighbors, corporations that choose not to partner fairly with other businesses, and governments that isolate themselves from the rest of the world.

For our own spiritual health and for the sake of the world, every one of us needs to be involved in a "goal community" — a group that strives toward a goal that is too large for any one individual in the group to meet. For scientists, it is discovering the truth about the way things work. For lawyers, it is upholding the law. For workers in a car factory, it is manufacturing cars. These goals are too large for just one person. Because they are so big, they demand self-transcendence.

Self-transcendence means allowing your soul's gifts to be used in the service of something larger than yourself. In his address on receiving the Philadelphia Liberty Medal, Václav Havel summarized the importance of self-transcendence (excerpted from the *New York Times*, 8 July 1994):

> Only someone who submits to the authority of the universal order and of creation, who values the right to be a part of it and a participant in it, can genuinely value himself and his neighbors and thus honor their rights as well.
>
> It follows that, in today's multicultural world, the truly reliable path to peaceful coexistence and creative cooperation must start from what is at the root of all cultures and what lies infinitely deeper in human hearts and minds than political opinion, convictions, antipathies or sympathies: it must be rooted in self-transcendence.

Finding the True Goal

One day as I was working in the technology division of a telephone company, I found a note on my desk. It said, "Our Division's Mission Statement: blah blah blah." At least that's what I remember it saying. I'm sure it said something about

being the best in   the market and delivering leading-edge
telecommunications billing technology and exceeding the
expectations of our "internal and external customers." I just

GOAL COMMUNITIES

Goal communities are groups of
people who are working toward a
larger goal, a task that demands
self-transcendence.

remember thinking that
whatever the mission was,
it didn't resonate with me.
In fact, I took an informal
poll, and no one felt like the
mission resonated with
them either.

The stated mission of the goal community in which we spent
ten of our sixteen waking hours every weekday did not resonate
with what we had to offer. Yet I (and others) consciously chose to
rejoin this community every day. Why? Because the stated mission of the goal community was wrong. The true goal was something else. The true goal of a community is not dictated to the
members of the community; it is defined by them.

Whenever the leaders of a religion, company, university,
nonprofit, or government try to define a goal for a community,
their dictated goal will be overridden by the true goal.
Sometimes the true goal is far loftier than the dictated goal, and
sometimes it's not as lofty. For example, sometimes in my
group the true goal was to make our division more peaceful and
friendlier. Our division existed in a world of meanness, and we
wanted to change that. We had pride in our work, but our work
was to make telephone-billing software. At these times our true
goal was loftier than just developing good software. At other
times the morale of the community was so low that even the
dictated mission was never reached. The true goal of the community became to screw over the leadership, create divisive-
ness in the ranks, or try to get nice severance packages.

The true goal of a goal community can either overwrite the
dictated goal or it can show the community exactly what needs
to be fixed so that a more worthwhile goal can become the true,
shared goal. But the true goal seems to have an evolutionary

force. It evolves from the gifts of everyone in the community; as old members leave and new ones join, the goal changes. The Goal-Blessing Ritual takes you through one way of working with your goal community to allow its true goal to emerge.

GOAL BLESSING

GOAL: *To help define or redefine the true goal of the community and reinvigorate the community's commitment to the goal*

What You'll Need:

- the current members of your goal community
- a room to contain them
- two to five hours
- a chalkboard, white board, or flip chart to write on
- paper and writing tools

1. Bring together as many members of the goal community that can reasonably come together. For a very large community, consider conducting several rituals.

2. Each member first takes some time to formulate, in her or his own mind, the blessings that she or he would like to offer for the goal of the community — that it may heal the earth, that it may increase love, and so on. These are not statements of the goal itself but rather blessings for the goal based on the gifts that come from each member. The members write down their blessing for the goal and put the papers in a pile. When everyone is ready, read the blessings.

3. Each member now formulates a description of what they see as the goal of the community. The goal descriptions might be something like: finding a

faraway star system, mapping the human genome in record time, developing better communication tools for the elderly, putting on a musical with a new kind of music, and so forth. Members write down their descriptions of the goal and put the papers in a pile. When everyone is ready, read the descriptions.

4. Spend some time in silence and feel what it is like to not have an agreed-on definition of the community's goal but to have a very blessed goal. Let the goal of the community form, while staying silent for at least five minutes. This step is crucial: The goal of the community needs time to form and should not be imposed on the community.

5. Each member now writes down (on her or his own piece of paper) the blessings and goal descriptions that resonated most strongly with her or him. These are not new blessings or descriptions but ones that have already been heard by the group. The members put their pieces of paper in a pile.

6. When everyone is ready, read the papers. As the blessings and descriptions are being read, keep track of each blessing and goal description by writing them somewhere that is accessible to everyone. When a blessing or goal description gets more than two mentions, circle that blessing or goal description.

7. Repeat Step Five, except now using the circled blessings and goal descriptions. Follow with Step Six, and keep repeating Steps Five and Six until the same goal descriptions and blessings keep reappearing without change for one full cycle.

8. Combine the blessing(s) and goal description(s) into one goal, such as "The goal of our community is to use our blessings of [blessing one], [blessing two], and [blessing three] to nurture the development of [goal one] and [goal two]."

9. As a closing, create a circle and stand. Silently imagine blessing the goal with everyone's gifts.

> NOTE: You might want to follow this ritual with
> the Repair Experiment (see end of chapter).

Choosing Your Goal Communities

Though your growth community is created for you, you can pick
and choose your goal communities. You probably already have
chosen at least one goal community: Maybe it's your job or your
yoga class, or maybe it's your synagogue, church, or mosque. It
could be your family or your marriage. When you consciously
choose your goal communities, you are drawn to goals that resonate with your purpose and your gifts. So in a healthy goal community, each person in the community will bring a unique
sense of purpose and make a unique impact on the goal.

When I was leading a group of software testers, our goal
was to make sure that the software we tested was accurate, efficient, and user friendly. According to the feedback we received,
our group met that difficult goal very well. But we only achieved
the goal through having a diverse array of people in our group.
I really enjoyed getting the software in line with where the
documentation said it was supposed to be — this resonated
with my purpose, which is about increasing truth. But another
equally important member of our group resonated with the
goal of the software itself: to test health-care diagnostic tools.
He used his gifts to ensure that the software met that end goal
efficiently, and his impact was to represent practical application
as a desirable virtue. He and I and the others in our group all
influenced different elements of the goal, which is what made
our group so successful when we acted together.

In nonfunctioning or unconscious goal communities, the
goal and everything else (process, requirements, rules for
membership) are up for grabs. When we choose our goal communities without consciousness, they seem to grind their

gears, forfeiting for us the experience of ever reaching the goal
and certainly never reaching the transformational experience of
self-transcendence.

I started a goal community at my university with the intention
of bringing together people who want to learn about how we can
make science a more human effort. To my surprise, chemists,
biologists, and even mechanical engineers showed up at the first
meeting. Three years later, the group is still going strong, working
hard on a book project. But even after we had done some signifi-
cant work on clarifying our goals, one member left the group.

It turns out that she had joined unconsciously; she had
joined to be near another group member that she liked. Once
she no longer had the crush, she decided to leave the group,
because her work did not resonate with our goal. We did not
begrudge her for leaving, but once she left we noticed that our
work on the book moved faster and took less effort.

Discovering that you've unconsciously joined a goal community can be as easy as asking yourself whether you consciously chose each community you are in or as difficult as
spending years banging your head against the wall every time
you work with certain people. However you do it, when you recognize a goal community that you joined without consciousness, your first task is to choose whether you will continue
to be a member of that community. Here are some questions
to ask about your goal communities:

- Does your work contribute toward the goal of the
  community? If not, investigate why you were drawn
  to it.
- Can you make a fully conscious choice to join the
  community? If not, you are most likely not able to
  benefit that goal community.
- Can you make a fully conscious choice to leave the
  community? If not, your gifts are needed
  within that goal community. Work on being able to
  make a fully conscious choice to join it.

Transformation and Transcendence

Emperor penguins endure snowstorms by forming slowly moving masses. Scientists who watch these circles have noticed that each penguin follows the same path in the mass — it will start on the outside of the mass and spiral inward to the center, then make its way out to the edge again. Field researchers reason that this kind of movement lets each penguin spend most of its time warmed by other penguins in the center of the mass. But they also notice that each penguin spends a little time in the cold, on the outside of the mass, to give the other penguins a chance to be in the center.

It might seem that these penguins sacrifice themselves for the welfare of the group. But that intuition turns out to be wrong. If the penguins were sacrificing their own comfort, that would mean they would be better off staying in the center of the mass, yet they choose instead to pursue a greater good and move toward the outside. But the truth is that being in the mass is the warmest place a penguin can be, and the mass moves. So there is no other option. The lesson for us is when we try to meet our needs the best we can, the way to both individual and group success is the same.

Within a functioning goal community, each member finds her or his own growth communities. This kind of camaraderie can be seen as petty "office politics," but it is neither petty nor political. It is an expression of the natural and healthy desire of our souls to connect with those who will further our growth. Wherever we are, when we work with the gifts our growth communities give us, we are transforming ourselves. That first repair is necessary for the second repair of self-transcendence; if we are not actively working on our growth, we will never be able to see past ourselves.

As we move closer to our goal, each member of the community is further transformed by the experience of transcending themselves to see the goal take shape. We have each followed our own paths, but now we find our paths meeting the paths that others have made. Once we've chosen to connect, share our gifts, and create, our paths no longer belong only to God and us; they belong to the world as well. To the extent that you allow your path to change as you work toward your creation, your creation itself will transform you.

RESISTANCE: A SHADOW TOOL

The leaders of large corporations complain that their employees are resistant to change. No matter how many books with illustrated fables they buy for their employees, somehow those darned people still don't want to change. At the same time, employees complain that the leaders of their companies are resistant to change. No matter how many times they tell their bosses that management is worthless, their bosses don't seem to listen. Both complaints are usually accurate. Resistance is like a wall — it always has two sides.

When we experience resistance, it tells us two things: 1) There is a force that we are blocking, and 2) We are afraid this force will hurt whatever is on the other side of the block. In the corporate example, the employees might feel that removing their walls of resistance will result in the force of change wiping out their seemingly fragile sense of purpose. The leaders also feel that removing their walls of resistance will result in the force of change coming from the other direction, destroying their seemingly fragile sense of purpose. Even though the employees have the same problem as the leaders, the resistance of both remains strong.

The force that we sense when we focus on our resistance is either the force of transformation or of transcendence. The fact that we experience resistance tells us that our goal community is healthy; we are experiencing the tension between self-transformation and self-transcendence. But we intuitively know that this force will cause turmoil and destruction if what is in its path is not strong enough to contain and shape it. The solution is to add strength to the other side of the force. When the pressure is equalized, we can remove the wall of resistance and the balance will restore itself.

Dorothy and Todd are in a romantic partnership. Dorothy is more likely than Todd to sacrifice herself for the sake of the relationship, and she gets upset at Todd because of this. Todd is more likely to sacrifice the relationship for his own needs — he'll choose to take time for himself when she needs time together, even when they've just been working hard all week. Dorothy feels confident in her own strength and resists the force that she fears might hurt the relationship, while Todd feels more confident in the relationship and feels he needs to protect himself.

In a sense, the wall of resistance is one we build at the boundary between our individual paths and the place where our paths meet our goal communities. Either we fear our own path is not strong and clear enough to handle the will of the community, or we fear the community does not have the strength to survive the power that lives within us. To use resistance for its true purpose, we must begin to see the strength that already exists on the weak side of the wall. Then we can add to that strength until we see that it can handle the force we fear.

THE RESISTANCE-RELEASING PRACTICE

GOAL: *To release resistance to transformation and resistance to transcendence by strengthening what we perceive as weak*

STEP ONE: *See your path as a river.*

Visualize a river of your soul's gifts flowing into an ocean, adding your gifts to those from your goal community. Also imagine the ocean influencing and drawing out the flow of your river. Now try to see the wall that blocks both of these flows, blocking both self-transcendence and self-transformation.

STEP TWO: *Be the wall.*

Imagine you are the wall of resistance. Ask yourself how you were built, who built you. Why are you here? What are you separating?

STEP THREE: *Be the river.*

Imagine you are the river. Ask yourself if you are capable of holding your own flow. Really explore the strength of your river, asking yourself how you can add to your strength.

STEP FOUR: *Be the ocean.*

Visualize yourself as the ocean, the continuous creation of your goal community. Ask yourself if you are strong and capable of maintaining your current even with a powerful river pouring into you. Really feel the power within yourself. Ask yourself how you can add to the strength of this ocean.

STEP FIVE: *Be the wall again.*

Go back to imagining yourself as the wall of resistance. Ask yourself if you are willing to be dissolved. If you are not, go back to Step One. If you are, allow yourself to feel both sides — the river that wants to flow into the ocean and the ocean that wants to influence the river — come together. Feel the renewed power that comes from joining these forces. This is the gift of resistance.

MEMBERSHIP: LEADERSHIP AND PARTICIPATION

We all know that some people who are named as leaders do not necessarily practice leadership, while some who claim they are "merely" participating seem to behave like leaders. Leadership and participation are not static labels for individuals but rather skills that each of us needs to balance in our goal communities. Membership in a goal community requires that we practice both leadership and participation.

The work of leadership is to see the beauty of the gifts in the community, to name and uphold the goal, and to stitch together the soul's work of each member of the community to continuously create the goal. Not easy. But the participant also has a tough job. Each participant must become fully conscious of her own purpose and how it influences the goal, make sure the stated goal resonates with her and if not change the goal or change communities, transform herself via her growth community, and be a leader of her own internal democracy so that the goal community gets her best possible work. Leaders foster the goal, while participants develop the individual gifts that help the goal community in its creation.

If we want to achieve optimal functioning of our goal communities, we will each find ourselves in both roles at different times. The motivations behind leadership and participation naturally balance the interconnected goals of transformation and transcendence. It is only when we balance our leading experiences with our participating experiences that we become active members of our goal communities.

When everyone in a goal community acts as a leader at some times and as a participant at others, resistance breaks down. Everyone experiences the strength and weaknesses of the community and of its members. Everyone knows the struggle of transcendence and of transformation. As resistance dissolves, so do our old fears that the goal will get twisted toward the whims of the leaders, or that the participants won't do their work.

When it's working well, the academic science community follows this model. To evaluate a grant for funding, a rotating review panel of scientists is selected to read and judge the grant. One year you may be one of these scientists, but the next year you may be trying to get a grant funded. As a reviewer, you know what the scientists have gone through to produce the grant proposals. As a scientist trying to be funded, you know (or you know someone who knows) what it is like to review hundreds of grants. The balance strengthens the goal of the community and at the same time supports everyone in developing their soul's work.

THE SECOND REPAIR: HEALING CREATION

We are all unique threads of a universal fabric. But too often we are trained to see ourselves as only these individual units: I am the yellow silk thread, you are the green wool yarn, he is the orange polyester fiber. And there is truth and importance in our uniqueness. But in only remembering our uniqueness, we can easily forget two things. First, we can forget that our lives are intimately entwined with the lives of others. The first repair, connection, heals this break (see chapter 5). Second, we can forget that we are all threads of the same fabric, all elements of the same tapestry. Healing creation, the second repair, reminds us again of the whole.

In a sense, the goal of any goal community can be seen as a child. The needs of the children foster self-transcendence in the parents and grandparents. At the same time, the children themselves transform the entire family. If we see our goals as children that we are raising to adulthood, we can more easily understand the healing that we are creating in the world. Healthy goal communities create a living, breathing thing that exists beyond the existence of anyone in the community or even the community itself. This entity is a healing creation of the community.

Just like children, the goal of a goal community is not without its troubles. The goal itself becomes an entity, with its own nature and purpose. It too must learn to discover, master, and share its own gifts. Just as with children, it is easy to forget that the goal has a life of its own, that it will go out and alter the world. It can also be easy to forget that we are at least partially responsible for the way the goal alters the world.

Healing creation has three meanings. Each meaning is essential for a healthy goal community. The first meaning is that our day-to-day creative efforts in our goal communities must be healing in themselves; the act of our creation must be healing. It is no good to house the homeless if within your non-profit you are constantly bickering. The second meaning is that our larger intention must be to heal the world itself, and we must always measure our actions with that ultimate goal; we must focus on healing all creation. The final meaning is that our goal must be to create something healing; a product, service, or process that serves to heal. The second repair will not happen if what we create is ultimately destructive.

Some of the Manhattan Project scientists who worked on the physics of the nuclear bomb felt that they could do their

---

THE THREE MEANINGS OF HEALING CREATION

- Creating in a healing way,
- Sharing the intention to heal all of creation,
- Creating a product, service, or process that is healing.

science without making a value judgment about the end goal. Their line was that pure science does not concern itself with application. The truth was that some of them were intrigued by the scientific problems, enjoyed the prestige and funding they found in the project, and wanted to rationalize their reasonable fears about building a very destructive weapon. It's possible that this group of scientists worked in harmony and felt that their creation would help heal the world. After all, they thought Hitler might develop an A-bomb before they could — ultimately, theirs could be seen as a protective act. But when Oppenheimer saw the first mushroom cloud, he quoted the Bhagavad Gita, saying, "I have become death, destroyer of worlds." He immediately recognized his group's fatal error — that their creation itself was not a healing one.

As we choose our goal communities with consciousness, we need to take the goals seriously. If they become entities in their own rights, how can we prepare them to move in a healing direction? What qualities do they need so we can love what they've become? How can we ensure that our goals operate as healing creations instead of as destructive ones? Had they asked these questions, the nuclear scientists may have instead done what Einstein did. He made discoveries that led to infinite possibilities, including destruction. Then he worked to educate and inspire scientists to use his answers to mend, not harm, the world.

How much we can love our creations tells us how well they can heal the world. To create as God has created us — and see that our creation is good — is the world repair our souls are here to make. At the same time, we must become parents who can see the value of parenting, even if the future does not include our children or us. We must see that love itself, the love moving from creator to creation, is the only thing that lasts. It is the only gift we can offer back to God.

THE REPAIR EXPERIMENT

GOAL: *To begin healing the world with our creations*

NOTE: Do this experiment alone in preparation for working with your goal community.

STEP ONE: *Experience your power and path.*
Find a quiet time. Ensure that you have little or no resistance to self-transcendence or to self-transformation (use the Resistance-Releasing Practice or another method). Imagine your unique, perfect light pouring from you as a river. When it is flowing well, imagine partnering with God to determine the path this river can take.

STEP TWO: *Meet with the paths of others.*
When your path is clear, see your river meeting with other rivers, exchanging light that transforms you and others. Visualize this transformed light flowing toward the creation of your goal community. Now imagine each member of your goal community experiencing the same flow of light. Visualize the beauty of this ocean that belongs to no one, the place into which your light and the light of everyone in your community flows.

STEP THREE: *Experience the nexus.*
Now visualize yourself walking, swimming, diving, flying, or somehow getting to the meeting point of your river of light with the ocean. Experience the power of this point. Record in your Unfolding Notebook the answers to these questions:

- What wisdom can I find in this place?
- What do I feel here?

- What do I know about myself?
- What do I know about healing the world?

STEP FOUR: *Bring the power to work with you.*
Spend at least five minutes letting this source of healing fill you as preparation for performing healing creation with your goal community. Go and work with your goal community, consciously drawing on this power as you work with others toward your shared goal.

CREATION

The plant is now full, harvested, and wilting. It allows each tendril, each waxy stalk, each rootlet to weaken and dry. Just as its fruits were used to feed the big animals, so will its stalks feed the small. The earth, too, is fed from its remains. Now it falls, now it dies. And so it lives.

What to include in your Unfolding Notebook:

- tools that help your goal communities work more consciously
- insights from the wall of resistance
- insights into your goal community
- results from the Repair Experiment
- awakenings you share with others

You know you have completed the work in this section when you have shared

- the evolution of community goals,
- your resistance and its lessons,
- roles of leader and participant, and
- an experience of healing creation.

SHARING SOUL MAP: THE WHOLE

GOAL: *To exchange the separateness necessary for our paths for the wholeness necessary to step outside them*

NOTE: Please know that every time the directions instruct you to "make a reminder," the idea is to draw, paint, write, paste fabric, or do whatever helps you to remember.

STEP ONE: *Gather your materials.*
Find a large surface to use for your map (you could try poster board, fabric, or cardboard). On this surface, you will create reminders of each of your communities and the whole they create. Have your Soul Maps and your Unfolding Notebook on hand.

STEP TWO: *Remember your purpose.*
On one side of the map, make a reminder of your purpose (see chapter 2 and your Discovery Soul Map). Around your purpose, make a reminder of the people in your resonant community (see chapter 1) who nourish and support you in your soul's work.

STEP THREE: *Remember your path and your partnership.*
Elsewhere on the map, make a reminder of your soul's path, including the challenges and insights it has already brought you (see chapter 4 and your Mastery Soul Map). Around this path, add reminders of your partnership with the Universe (see chapter 3).

STEP FOUR: *Remember the two repairs.*
In another place on the map, create reminders of the gifts you have shared with members of your

growth community (see chapter 5). Surround this area with the goal communities that depend on these gifts (see chapter 6). Also in this area make a reminder of the healing creation you've done or intend to do with your goal communities (see the Repair Experiment, this chapter).

STEP FIVE: *Remember the whole.*

Unite all three reminder areas by encircling them with reminders of your commitments to yourself, God, and others. Include reminders of at least three things you commit to doing to support your work, and at least three things you can ask from others. Take a moment to bless your map.

MAY WE JOIN TOGETHER IN LOVE!

EPILOGUE

Return

In wholeness, we see that we are not the water, but the river, not the path but the journey itself. At the same moment some part of us is starting out, facing danger, another part is being healed, experiencing transformation and transcendence. As one part becomes lost, another part is finding a new way. Because we have chosen to consciously experience our unfolding, we now know our journey intimately. We can use this knowledge and apply it to our future paths. In this way, we can put aside some of our suffering and replace it with hard-won joy.

Now that you have claimed your unfolding as your own, your soul knows what is coming, what you've left behind, and what will come again. Because we each have made the tools we need, we can commit to using them for our future unfolding. We are on this path for all time, but this path is no longer what it once was. It has become part of you. You can enjoy using your unfolding again, in another way, and another way, forever.

THE HANDBOOK EXPERIMENT

GOAL: *To turn your Unfolding Notebook into an Unfolding Handbook — a place to consult for insights, help, and guidance for your future work and play*

STEP ONE: *Organize your notebook.*

Gather your Unfolding Notebook — if it has any loose papers, bind them somehow. Make sure that your notebook is complete and that it includes all your unfolding notes. Don't worry if you didn't do every practice, ritual, meditation, or experiment you wanted to do. Just get what you have together and let yourself call it your Unfolding Notebook.

STEP TWO: *Mark important sections.*

Use tabs, highlighter, stickers, folded-down pages — whatever works — to mark the major sections of your notebook. These sections might be defined by the parts or chapters of this book, or you might split up your notebook based on feelings or major shifts in your unfolding. You may not have any sections. Just consider whether there is a natural way to divide up your notebook that might prove helpful in the future.

STEP THREE: *Revisit each section.*

Spend some time walking through the notebook, rereading each section. You might pay special attention to your Soul Maps. What did each part teach you? What were the most important and useful tools you found? How did you get stuck and what got you unstuck? What would you tell yourself now if you were facing the problems that you faced in each section? In the future, how could you best use the information in each section?

STEP FOUR: *Write these insights down.*

Either on a summary page at the end of your notebook,

on individual loose-leaf pages placed in each section, or with some other method, write down the insights you gained.

STEP FIVE: *Let your notebook become your handbook.* Add anything else you think you may need to make this handbook something that you will enjoy using in your future unfolding. Add photos, drawings, songs, poems — whatever would make this a handbook you will treasure and use. As you move along your path, return to your handbook and add pages as you need, developing new sections or adding on to old ones. Let the handbook grow as your exploration deepens.

Change and love are the two most powerful forces in the universe. Together, they create our unfolding. Love is the material out of which we are made, and the matrix in which we live. There is nothing else to us. Since there is no division in love, the only thing love can do is change. The disappointments, joys, and concerns in our lives are really just shadows of love doing a changing dance. The rhythms of our unfolding are the rhythms of love, dancing through its changes.

RETURN

The plant feels itself under sand and gritty dirt, sleeping before the spring. It has known fruit, it has given life. Now it is strong. It knows itself in the soil, in the birds that peck overhead, in the neighboring roots and rocks. In relief, it finds itself small, quiet, at home under the soil. There is nothing left to do. And it will begin again.

A LABORATORY TOOL KIT

A Laboratory Tool Kit

RESOURCES FOR PART ONE: DISCOVER

Chapter One: Nature

"Here I am."

(The ancient phrase used by many mystics, this meditation centers you in your source.)

"This is my nature."

(This meditation is useful if you have the urge to pin down your nature rather than letting it shift and move over time. Repeating *this* over again helps you draw attention to what is happening right now.)

"I am perfect."

(A simple reminder that there is no other way to be than how you are right now.)

"Source."

(This meditation can help you draw energy from your source.)

THE MIRROR

GOAL: *To experience being in your nature while there is a big distracter (the mirror) in front of you*

STEP ONE: *See your reflection.*
Set a watch or timer for five minutes and find a private room with a mirror. Look at yourself in the mirror for five minutes. Try different expressions — surprise, anger, fear, joy — and also try relaxing your face. Just keep looking no matter how easily you become distracted. If you get distracted, look back into the mirror.

STEP TWO: *See yourself.*
Let yourself feel what it's like to just be inside yourself, not in the mirror image. Can you place your awareness inside your own body, not in the mirror image? When you can, what does your reflection look like to you?

A PIECE OF GOD

GOAL: *To remind you that your source is a piece of Love*

STEP ONE: *See your source outside you.*
Stand up and relax your body, including your shoulders. Keep your eyes open. Now imagine, in front of you, a ball of love. Let this ball look however it does — later you can write down how it appeared to you.

STEP TWO: *Choose your source.*

Imagine God giving you this ball as a gift; imagine the ball coming from God and moving toward you. Notice if you have any concerns about or resistance to the ball. If so, let them be there. Ask yourself whether you will let the ball come into your body.

STEP THREE: *Learn about your source.*

If the ball is outside you, commit to discovering why you feel you must choose to leave the ball outside you. Then commit to retrieving the ball when you are ready. If you let the ball inside, feel it bounce around. Play with the ball a while. Is it small or large? What color is it? What is it made of? Let yourself blur your boundaries with the ball, so that it fills every cell of your body. What does this feel like?

SOURCE CRADLING

GOAL: *To actively love your source*

STEP ONE: *Be in your source.*

Locate your source in your body — just let your hands move to where you imagine the center of your source might be. Put your hands over your source and breathe deeply. Say to yourself, "Here I am," or use another meditation for centering yourself in your source.

STEP TWO: *See your source.*

Concentrate on what is underneath your hands. Notice if an image or word comes up to represent what is beneath your hands. You could see an old rotting tomato, a beautiful sunflower, or the word *sand*. Just let all images or words come up. Notice what comes up most strongly, and let that image or word stay.

STEP THREE: *Love your source.*

Watch or listen to your image or word as you say to it, "I love you." Keep repeating "I love you" as the image or word shifts.

STEP FOUR: *Feel your source.*

Now, taking your hands away, let yourself feel your source as it is now. Record in your notebook the word or image that came up and how it shifted. What does the shift tell you?

YOUR NATURAL ELEMENTS

GOAL: *To discover the recurring elements of your nature and to investigate any elements that don't feel natural to you*

STEP ONE: *Brainstorm.*

List in your Unfolding Notebook the elements of your nature that you already know appear in your everyday life. Here is a partial list to get you started:

activist	judge	stalwart
actor	knower	student
artist	leader	teacher
catalyst	magician	thinker
connoisseur	mediator	tinkerer
dreamer	nourisher	uniter
explorer	peacemaker	visionary
facilitator	pleaser	wanderer
feeler	rabble-rouser	whiner
fixer-upper	scientist	wonderer
follower	seer	
healer	speaker	

STEP TWO: *Take it on the road.*

Spend a good chunk of your day reminding yourself to ask what element your nature is expressing right now. Jot each one down on your list.

STEP THREE: *Sort the elements.*

Once you are convinced that you have listed most of the recurring elements of your nature, sit down with your list. Looking at each element, ask yourself if it is a true expression of your nature or whether it is a character that you play. If it is a character, ask yourself when this character appears and why. The next time the character appears, see if you can let yourself get to the underlying reason for that character getting in the way of the true expression of your nature.

STEP FOUR: *Celebrate your nature!*

As you look at the list of elements in your nature, imagine each one as a separate person. Choose one small practical thing you can do to celebrate all the elements of your nature (bring them all to dinner, your treat? make silly hats for all of them? give each of them a small present?). Imagine what kind of work these people could do together, what kind of fun they could have, and what conversations might be like if they were all in a room at once.

PLANTING I

GOAL: *To create a physical reminder*
of your unfolding

NOTE: At the end of this tool kit, there is a second
planting ritual that incorporates the plants you will
grow in this ritual.

What You'll Need:

- a half hour set aside
- your Unfolding Notebook
- something to write with
- potting soil
- a place to plant (flowerpot, outdoor garden, or
  flowerboxes)
- seeds to plant

1. Before you plant, do some research on how the
    seeds will grow best. Find a place to plant them
    where they will have enough light and moisture
    and where the temperature is right for them. Write
    these conditions in your Unfolding Notebook. At
    the same time, write down what conditions you feel
    you might need for your unfolding.

2. Gather your planting supplies and get ready to
    plant the seeds. In your Unfolding Notebook, write
    down your hopes for these seeds, as well as your
    hopes for your unfolding. Record what you will do
    if something happens to the seeds so that their
    growth is thwarted: Will you transplant them?
    Plant new seeds? Buy young plants? Also record
    what you will do if something blocks your unfolding.

3. Plant the seeds, telling them your wishes as you plant them. Make a commitment to give them the growing environment they need. At the same time, make a commitment to yourself to give yourself what you need as you unfold.

4. As your unfolding continues, come back often to nurture the growing plants. As you do, use this time as a reminder to nurture yourself.

NAMING YOURSELF

GOAL: *To get insight into and play with your nature by choosing a name for yourself*

What You'll Need:

- ten minutes set aside
- your Unfolding Notebook
- something to write with
- a private place
- a word-game set, children's ABC toy or flash cards, or another representation of the alphabet (you can write out the alphabet for yourself if you like)
- a sense of humor and playfulness

1. Breathe deeply and get comfortable with yourself.

2. Blindly select a letter of the alphabet and meditate on it. Ask your name to come to you. (If it doesn't start with this letter, that's okay — these letters are just tools to stimulate your creativity.)

3. Be welcoming of all names, even if they don't seem like names. Politree, Replicon, Doolittle — these may not seem like reasonable (or beautiful) names at all, but each may have something to tell you about your nature in this moment.

4. Allow the name that you can't get out of your mind

to stick around. Say it out loud, write it down, turn it over and play with it. What message does it have for you?

5. Record your name and its message in your note-book.

THE SUCCESS RITUAL

GOAL: *To celebrate what you've already accomplished and prepare for your future*

What You'll Need:

- a half hour set aside
- your Unfolding Notebook
- a piece of paper and something to write with
- a stamped, self-addressed envelope
- a flower (bought or found)

1. Go for a walk and find a beautiful, semiprivate place. Sit down and write your "success story" in your Unfolding Notebook. Write it from the point of view that where you are right now is already a success. Don't worry about length; your story can be one sentence long if you like. You may want to answer these questions, or some of your own:

- How did you feel before you got here?
- What is this place like?
- What are you proud of in your journey here?
- What do you wish for the future?

2. Now write your success stories from the point of view of your destination. Even if you don't know where you're going, imagine that you do and that you are already there. In your success story, you may want to answer the same questions as above, or add some of your own.

3. Read the stories to yourself (or to the flower, if you like). Put the stories in the envelope and send them to yourself. Leave the flower behind to spread your success into the world.

4. When you receive the stories in the mail, ask your self how you are supporting your path.

ONLY RESONANCE

GOAL: *Letting go of things and/or people that don't resonate with your nature*

What You'll Need:

- ten minutes set aside
- a collection of things that don't resonate with your nature
- a box into which all these things will fit
- a plan to donate or recycle the contents of the box

1. After having done the Truth Experiment in chapter 1 several times, notice who does not resonate with your nature. These are people who don't support you, though once they may have.

2. For each nonresonating object, assign a non-resonating person until each nonresonating person is represented. You can have more nonresonating objects than you have people.

3. With the box on one side of you and the objects on the other, pick up each object. Hold the object and meditate on it. What did it give you? What did the person whom it represents give you? What blessing can you give the person it represents?

4. Once you are complete with the object, if you still decide to let go of it, put it in the box. As you do, imagine the object and the person it represents

drifting peacefully out of your environment
immediately.

5. If you change your mind and wish to reclaim the
    person it represents, ask what you can do to fully
    receive that person back into your life while still
    supporting your nature. Then place the object in a
    special place in your home.

6. Keep going until all the objects are either reclaimed
    or in the box. Then donate the box to the charity you
    selected, or recycle the contents.

Chapter Two: Purpose

MEDITATIONS

"Nothing is broken."

(This meditation is for reminding yourself that you don't need to do anything special to fulfill your purpose.)

"My power is my purpose."

(This is to remind you that the way to fulfill your purpose is to bring your power to the world.)

"I am loved for free."

(This meditation might be for you when you are convinced that you must justify your existence with your purpose.)

"My power needs me to claim it."

(Say this to remind yourself to receive your power back into your source.)

PRACTICES

RECEIVING COMPLIMENTS

GOAL: *To experience receiving fully without immediately needing to give anything in return*

NOTE: Do this practice only in the presence of a supportive person or supportive people.

STEP ONE: *Receive a compliment.*

Your trigger for doing this practice depends on receiving a compliment that matters to you. If someone you don't trust compliments your speaking style, and neither the person nor your speaking style is important to you, this is not the time. But when someone you trust compliments your shoes, and both that person and your shoes are important to you, this is the time for it.

STEP TWO: *Receive your power.*

After you hear the compliment, slowly count to ten. Breathe in and out several times and get in touch with your source. Imagine receiving your power with every cell of your body. Do not say or do anything else during the count to ten.

STEP THREE: *Notice your reaction.*

Notice if it is difficult for you not to return the compliment quickly or thank the giver. Just be with your discomfort and keep receiving your power.

STEP FOUR: *Respond.*

Say and do what feels natural to you; a simple "thank you," a hug, a handshake, or a return compliment might feel best.

THE WALL OF ANGER

GOAL: *To play with anger so you can discover what truths it is hiding from you*

STEP ONE: *Face the wall.*

Imagine yourself facing a wall of your own anger. Make the wall as angry as you like. Don't forget hostile graffiti or barbed wire, if they seem right. Imagine pounding it and wailing against it.

STEP TWO: *See the other side.*

When you are done imagining yourself banging against this wall, imagine that you are walking along it. Keep walking until you find the edge of the wall. Now walk around the wall to the other side. What do you see? Let yourself really take in what is on the other side of the wall. What was the wall separating you from? What does the wall look like on this side?

STEP THREE: *Create a path.*

Walk back to the other side of the wall and see what happens. Keep going back and forth, visiting both sides of the wall, until you've made a well-worn and comfortable path between them. The next time your anger flares up, imagine taking your path to the other side of the wall, and see what happens.

POWER FOCUSING

GOAL: *To practice focusing the power that comes from doing the Power Experiment*

STEP ONE: *Do the Power Experiment.*

Receive your power. Afterward, notice how it feels to have extra power in your source and all the light streaming out.

STEP TWO: *Find a fulfilling action.*

Wonder to yourself what the most fulfilling action would be for you right now. What would strengthen your source and support your purpose? Really be wide open on this one — don't limit it to what you would normally do this time of day, or what you've done before.

STEP THREE: *Bless your action.*

When you've found an action that feels right, go do it. While you do it, imagine focusing all your light on the action, blessing it with your light.

EXAMPLE: If your action is mending a sock, imagine focusing all your light on picking up the sock, threading the needle, and piercing the sock with the needle.

STEP FOUR: *Feel your light.*

When the action feels complete, love and appreciate what you have done. Love and appreciate your
light. Record in your notebook whether focusing
your power felt different from just doing the action
without focusing.

SHINING

GOAL: *To practice expressing your nature with
all the power that belongs to you*

STEP ONE: *Remember your source.*

Let yourself relax. Make yourself at home in your
nature, using the Yes Practice or another practice
to remember who you are right now.

STEP TWO: *Activate your source.*

Stay still and imagine yourself magnetically col-
lecting all the pieces of your source you have put in
other places: at work, at home, around people you
know, wherever your lost power is. Join this col-
lected power with your source. Enjoy the feeling of
all the power that truly belongs to you. (Thanks to
Garrett Walters, Spiritual Mechanic, for this step.)

STEP THREE: *Shine.*

Let your activated source shine — imagine light,
water, or energy coming from your source and
shining in all directions. Let yourself feel the infinite nature of your source, and see if you can catch
a glimpse of the goodness in the power you are
spilling out into the world.

STEP FOUR: *Shine actively.*

For at least five minutes, do the first thing that
occurs to you. Let it be whatever occurs to you —
no stipulations about saving the world or being

useful. Notice if you have the impulse to get distracted by something during those five minutes. Have the impulse and let yourself continue doing what you are doing anyway.

STEP FIVE: *Notice what happens.*

Write down how you feel now and what you discovered. Did any feelings come up when you were in your source? Where did you find pieces of your source? What did you do when you were shining actively? What does this tell you about your purpose right now?

> RITUALS

ANTIPASSION

GOAL: *To play with the energy of your passion*

What You'll Need:

- ten minutes set aside
- your notebook and something to write with
- a lighthearted mood
- a private place where you can run around

1. Before you start, get a sense of your passion. Now imagine what the opposite of your passion would be: What would it be like to do your "antipassion"?

2. Run around the room pantomiming things that are the opposite of your passion. If your passion is to bring people together, pantomime separation. If your passion is to make delicious food, pantomime burning everything on the stove.

3. Let yourself play with your antipassion. As you do, feel the energy of your passion countering every thing you pantomime.

4. When you are done, run around the room in the opposite direction, undoing all the antipassion work you just did. What does it feel like to imagine coming from your passion again?

5. Record in your notebook how it felt to work with your antipassion. Could you feel the energy of your passion trying to turn things the other way? What does this tell you about trying to make your passion something it isn't?

THE TURNING WHEEL

GOAL: *To begin to shift your awareness from fulfilling your purpose to moving on your soul's path*

What You'll Need:

- fifteen minutes set aside
- your Unfolding Notebook
- something to write with
- a bicycle and helmet
- a bike path or other safe place to ride

1. Before you start out, sit down and look at your bicycle. Imagine that the wheels represent the way you translate your passion into action and your actions into power. Look back at your Discovery Soul Map or the notes in your notebook to remind yourself exactly how your purpose process works.

2. Start riding slowly. Try to place your awareness in the wheels as you ride. What does it feel like to have to keep turning to move forward? What does it feel like to grip the road?

3. Now shift your awareness from the wheels to where you are, on the bicycle seat. What does it feel like to be able to guide the wheels wherever you want to go?

4. Keep switching your awareness, investigating how you make this switch. As you shift back and forth, also imagine yourself moving between the work of fulfilling your purpose and the larger work of guiding your purpose, and let yourself feel the value in both.

5. Finally, shift your awareness to riding the bicycle. Let yourself trust the wheels to turn around and around as they will, and see where the bicycle takes you.

THE LESSON OF THE SHIELD

GOAL: *To examine what resonates with your nature*

What You'll Need:

- ten minutes set aside
- your Unfolding Notebook
- something to write with
- a supportive person or group of supportive people
- an object held by each person

1. Imagine a flexible shield surrounding you, creating a safe boundary for your source. This shield lets love in and out of your source.

2. Once you are aware of your shield, ask someone to pass you his or her object. As you reach for the object, imagine your shield coming with you, surrounding your hand. As you hold the object, imagine that your shield is still surrounding your hand, beneath the object.

3. Allow yourself to extend the shield so that it encloses the object. How does it feel to have the object inside your shield? Now make your shield come underneath the object again. How does that feel?

4. Keep switching the position of your shield until you really have a sense of how each position feels. Then ask for another object, and start again.

5. When you have played with all the objects, make a note in your Unfolding Notebook about which objects (if any) felt best inside your shield and which objects (if any) felt best outside your shield. The objects you enjoy feeling inside your shield are the ones that resonate with you. What is the meaning of each object that resonated with you?

RESOURCES FOR PART TWO: MASTER

Chapter Three: Faith

MEDITATIONS

"I need God."

(This may be for you if you are stuck in the faith/fear dance on the side of "there probably is no God.")

"God needs me."

(This meditation unsticks you from the faith/fear dance when you are stuck on the side of "I am not good enough for God.")

"I know my God."

(Say this to remind yourself that you are the one who knows the God of your heart, even when your version of God is underrepresented in the world.)

"I fear _____ and _____."

(Fill in the first blank with what you fear and the second with that fear as a reality. As in, "I fear knowing God and I know God." This meditation is excellent for facing your fears.)

"I am allowed to ask."

(This one may be for you if you feel you don't have the right to do the Asking Experiment in chapter 3.)

EMPTY AND FULL

GOAL: *To ask God to fill you up with love*

STEP ONE: *Clear yourself out.*

Breathe deeply and imagine everything in you falling onto the floor. Everything is being washed down, as if there is a river that begins at your head and flows through the soles of your feet.

STEP TWO: *Feel the emptiness.*

Take a minute and feel empty. If you cannot feel entirely empty, that is understandable, because you aren't! Just feel whatever feelings of emptiness you can.

STEP THREE: *Notice what's left.*

Keep breathing deeply and notice what is left inside you. It could be a backache, a feeling of loneliness, a thought about tomorrow or whatever. Just notice what is left and allow it to be there.

STEP FOUR: *Ask God to fill you with love.*

Keep allowing what is left to be there, but at the same time, ask God to let the river start flowing from your head through your feet. This river is clear and clean and brings nothing with it but light and love. You do not need to let it wash anything away — rather, this river is filling you up along with whatever is already in you. Record how it feels to play with God in this way.

SPOT OF GOOD

GOAL: *To fill yourself up with love*

STEP ONE: *Find a spot of goodness.*

Close your eyes and take a quick internal look at your body. Find one spot in your body that you feel good about and that feels loose and free. (Even if it's your hair, that's okay!) Focus on the feelings of goodness in that spot.

STEP TWO: *Broaden the goodness.*

Let yourself broaden the goodness around that area. After all, the cells touching the "good spot" must be pretty good too, right? Keep broadening the goodness until it goes in all directions and keeps spreading. Let the goodness slowly become love.

STEP THREE: *Fill yourself up.*

Let your entire self be filled with love. This doesn't mean that you need to feel good about your whole body or that your whole body has to be pain free, healthy, or thin. It just means that the love has now spread completely, to permeate whatever else you feel in other parts of your body. Are you able to feel your whole self filled with love? If so, what does it feel like? If not, what areas of your body don't seem to receive the love? Ask God to fill these areas up and see if you can receive love from God.

GOD WALK

GOAL: *To get a better sense of the God of your heart*

STEP ONE: *Find a starting place.*

Go somewhere where you can walk without a destination for ten minutes. You are about to go on a walk with God at your side. During this walk you will get to know more about how you experience your God.

STEP TWO: *Walk with God.*

Start to walk. Feel God to your left side, to your right side, in front of you, and behind you. Where do you experience God most easily? Ask God to move around to other positions so you can feel Her in each place. Ask Her to show you where to walk and what to do next.

STEP THREE: *Let God take the lead.*

Let yourself walk where God shows you, and do what God asks you. See if you feel silly or uncomfortable as you are doing this. If you get stuck, say, "God! Where should I go? What should I do?"

STEP FOUR: *Go back to the beginning.*

Let yourself stop the walk when five minutes have passed. As you walk back to your starting place, experiment with having God come back with you as well. Record where it was easiest and hardest to feel God and any insights this gives you about your relationship with God. If you felt God most easily ahead of you, do you consider God your leader? What about behind you — does God hold you up? If God most easily walked beside you, do you see God as a sister or brother? Record how it felt to walk where God showed you and do what God asked you.

FOOT WASHING

GOAL: *To discover what you'd like to ask for in the Asking Experiment*

What You'll Need:

- a half hour set aside
- your Unfolding Notebook
- something to write with
- a place to wash: bathtub, shower, hose, or wash basin
- optional: a kind friend to wash your feet!

1. Sit near your washing place and close your eyes. Imagine you are about to ready yourself for a long journey. But first, you must gather your strength and resources for the trip ahead.

2. Without thinking too much, name at least three of the resources that have helped you get to where you are now. Open your eyes and wash your feet (or ask your friend to wash your feet). As your feet are touched gently and lovingly, imagine those resources being rubbed into your feet and moving through your body.

3. Now walk a bit, imagining that you have set out on your journey, bringing your resources with you. Imagine using each of the resources on your path. Also imagine picking up more resources on the way. What are these new resources?

4. Imagine yourself coming to a stopping place on your path. Wash your feet again (or ask your friend to). As your feet are again washed, imagine all the resources moving through your body.

5. After you dry off, record your resources and write

down which resources you want to ask for in the Asking Experiment. Pick small objects to represent each of them, and carry these with you for a while.

GREETING THE PATH

GOAL: *To celebrate where you are on your path*

What You'll Need:

- a half hour alone
- an interesting walking path
- your Unfolding Notebook
- something to write with
- a basket or similar object

1. With your basket, gather several small objects that seem important to you, but not priceless.
2. Take your basket on a walk, following the route that interests you. As you walk, let yourself leave each of the objects in places where you are likely to retrieve them later.
3. As you take each object from the basket and place it on your path, say a few words to yourself about the object. What is special about it? How does it feel to lend this object to your path?
4. Once all the objects are gone, keep walking. Now that your basket is empty, you can receive what your path offers. Find several gifts on your path — not the ones you put there, but new objects. These could be leaves, discarded wrappers, pinecones, or shells — whatever you are drawn to.
5. As you put each of these new objects in your basket, say a few words about them. Ask yourself why you were drawn to them. What new insights do they give you?
6. Now reverse your route. You will come across the

objects you originally brought with you. As you find
them, return them to your basket. Once you return
to your starting place, record what you discovered
in your Unfolding Notebook.

DANCING WITH GOD

GOAL: *To play with the idea of partnership
with God*

What You'll Need:

- ten minutes set aside
- your Unfolding Notebook
- something to write with
- a private place
- a source of music that fits your mood
- a luxurious outfit

1.   Get in your outfit and go to your private place.
     Don't turn on the music yet! Stand in the middle of
     the room and imagine God, in front of you, asking
     you to dance. How do you feel? Do you accept?
     Keep talking with God until you accept the dance
     under conditions that work for you.
2.   Now turn on the music and begin to dance with
     God — that is, move to the music and imagine God
     moving with you. Let God lead sometimes, and see
     how that feels. Then when you feel ready for a
     switch, see how it feels to lead God. What kind of
     movements are you doing in this dance? Are they
     familiar or unfamiliar?
3.   When you are ready to finish the dance, let God
     know how you enjoyed dancing with Him. Then be
     quiet and listen to find out how God felt. Let God
     give you a parting gift, and in exchange, give some-
     thing to God. Write about the dance and the gifts
     you exchanged in your Unfolding Notebook.

Chapter Four: Choice
MEDITATIONS

"I have chosen _____. Now I choose _____."
(Fill in the first blank with what you have chosen in the past. Fill in the second blank with what you now choose.)

"I choose what I am doing now."
(This is a reminder that no matter what has happened to you in the past, you are responsible for what you choose now.)

"This is the path of my soul."
(When you do this meditation, you'll quickly be able to tell whether it resonates truthfully. If it doesn't, meditate some more and ask where you need to change your path.)

"I do my work by playing with God."
(This one is for those of us who think everything worthwhile has to take effort and be serious.)

PRACTICES

CLEANING THE PATH
GOAL: *To ready your soul's path for your journey*

STEP ONE: *Envision the entrance to your path.*
   Sit down and relax your body. Close your eyes and let yourself imagine your soul's path in front of you. See the doorway to your soul's path. What does it look like? Also notice if the door is open or closed and whether anything blocks the entrance. Ask yourself how you can move anything that prevents you from entering.

STEP TWO: *Choose to enter.*
   Make a conscious choice to move whatever blocks the door. Once the way has been cleared, look for

anything else that prevents your movement, and repeat this step until everything is out of your way.

STEP THREE: *Enter.*

Walk toward the doorway and look through it. What do you see? Cross the threshold into your soul's path. Record in your Unfolding Notebook what was in your way, how you moved it, and what your path looked like after you stepped onto it.

ONE CHANGE

GOAL: *To take responsibility for one choice you have made*

STEP ONE: *Pick a choice.*

Sit down and relax your body. Look around your environment, wherever you are right now. If you had the power to change one thing you see or feel around you, what would that change be? This thing can be small, like doing your dishes. But you can also challenge yourself to pick something bigger, like changing your apartment or job.

STEP TWO: *Choose to change.*

Consciously choose to change this thing. If you are sure you choose to change it, take one action toward changing it. Complete it now. Once you have completed that action, how do you feel? What's the next thing you want to change?

PATH JUMPING

GOAL: *To visit other parts of your path to gain insight into where you are right now*

STEP ONE: *Visualize your path within you.*
Imagine that your whole path is within you. Locate in the path where you are right now. What is happening? How do you feel? Are you lost? In danger? Surrounded by people?

STEP TWO: *Ask your path what you need.*
Use the wisdom of your path to tell you what insights you could use right now. Let your path take you to another point on the path — in the past or the future. Go ahead and "jump" over whatever lies in between where you are now and where you are going. You will get to experience what lies between; right now you are just jumping the path to borrow the insights you need.

STEP THREE: *Listen to your path.*
Where did your path take you? What do you experience there? How does this relate or add to your experience in your original location?

STEP FOUR: *Jump back.*
Return to your original place on the path, the place where you were in Step One. What is it like now? Has anything changed? Are you moving well? Did your insights help? If not, go back to Step One and keep working with this practice until you get what you need.

PLAYING WITH CHOICE

GOAL: *To spark your creativity about the choices you have in your life*

What You'll Need:

- twenty minutes set aside
- your Unfolding Notebook
- something to write with
- a private place with a chair

1. Sit and write in your Unfolding Notebook a list of at least ten choices you don't have. For example, the list could include whether to go to the mall yesterday, whether you should be shorter or taller, what your mother's name should be, and so on. Force yourself to make sure each choice is one you really can't have.

2. Now allow yourself to imagine that you have all of the choices on the list. Move down the list, choice by choice, and write down what you choose. Let yourself really feel what choice is right for you, if you had it.

3. Make another list right next to the first one. This is a list of related choices, choices you do have. For instance, if the first choice on your list is whether to go to the mall yesterday, the related choice could be whether you choose to go to the mall today. Make sure you really have all these choices.

4. Now ask God to join you in moving down the second list, choice by choice; consult Him on each choice. Do the Path Experiment, in chapter 4, if you like. What do you choose? Does God have an opinion too? When you are done with the lists, ask for God's help in your future choices.

SHARED-RESPONSIBILITY WALK

GOAL: *To practice sharing responsibility with God*

What You'll Need:

- one hour
- your Unfolding Notebook
- a piece of paper you can rip up
- something to write with
- walking weather

1. Rip up the piece of paper into ten or twenty pieces. On each piece, write instructions to yourself. Choose things that would not make you too uncomfortable in public (for example, "get naked and dance" might be a hard one).

   EXAMPLE: Smile at a stranger, hug your mother, eat a peach, knock at a door, sing your favorite song.

2. Put the pieces of paper in your pocket or purse, then gather your things to go for a walk.

3. As you walk, pay attention to any peculiar events — I'll call them "signs." Signs might be a feeling you have inside yourself, such as a desire to laugh; something you hear, like a siren; or something you see or feel, like a falling leaf.

4. Each time you receive a sign, pick up one piece of paper and read the instructions. Follow the instructions as well as you can.

5. Once you feel the walk is complete, take out a final piece and notice where it takes you. Record in your Unfolding Notebook anything you discovered along your path, especially your insights about uncertainty, responsibility, and discovery.

HOME BUILDING

GOAL: *To create a physical reminder of your soul's path*

What You'll Need:

- a half-hour alone
- your Unfolding Notebook
- something to write with
- to be at your home

1. Without cleaning anything up, walk through your home as it is right now. Enter through your front door, then go to each room in turn. As you walk through each room, ask yourself how you use it, then write your answer(s) in your Unfolding Notebook.

2. For example, you use your bedroom to sleep. But you also use it for writing, playing with the cat, and practicing the banjo. Then you would write sleep, writing, cat petting, and banjo strumming next to "bedroom" in your notebook.

3. After you've finished, close your eyes and mentally move through your home again. Room by room, imagine what each would look like if you could remodel the rooms in any way you wanted. Record how you would use each of these new, improved rooms.

4. How you fantasize about remodeling your home shows what you are working toward in your unfolding. Would you add an observatory or a rooftop tennis court? Then you may be working toward opening up more space to learn or play. Would you add an indoor garden? You might be moving toward getting more in touch with the earth.

5. In closing, choose one small symbol of the changes
    you'd like to make and place that in your home. For
    example, you might create a plant corner in your
    kitchen if you fantasize about an indoor garden.
    Every time you see your symbol, imagine moving
    toward what it represents.

CONVERSATION WITH LOSS

GOAL: *To discover what your loss can teach you*

What You'll Need:

- fifteen minutes set aside
- your Unfolding Notebook
- something to write with
- a private place
- two chairs

1. Sit in one of the two chairs. First, you will become
    your loss. Imagine you are sitting in the other chair.
    As your loss, tell the "you" in the other chair exactly
    why you feel loss. Don't forget anything — all sad
    and longing feelings are fair game. When loss is
    done, move to the other chair.

2. Now you are facing loss. First, take in everything
    loss has said. Once you have remembered every-
    thing loss said, see if you can feel it. How does it
    feel?

3. Tell loss how it feels to hear all this. Tell loss about
    any feelings you have.

4. Move back to the other chair, as loss, and share any
    reactions. Go back to your chair and receive the
    reactions. Share any responses you have. Keep
    switching chairs until everything is said.

5. Put both chairs away. Stand up in the middle of the

room and ask your loss to return to being part of
you. Spend a moment with this returning part
of you, maybe dancing or moving. In your
Unfolding Notebook, record the highlights of your
conversation.

RESOURCES FOR PART THREE: SHARE

Chapter Five: Connection

MEDITATIONS

"I am a healer."
(This is a reminder that as we share our gifts, we heal oth-
ers and ourselves.)
"I am ready to share."
(Say this one to open yourself to sharing gifts with others.)
"I love and protect my gifts."
(This reminds you not to separate yourself from your gifts.)
"Judgment is fear of myself."
(This is a reminder that judgment tells us what part of us
needs love and acceptance.)

PRACTICES

HANDS 1

GOAL: *To celebrate the transformational space
between two people*

STEP ONE: *Find a partner.*
Find a partner who is included in your growth
community and who includes you in his or her
growth community. Both partners should keep
silent until Step Three.

STEP TWO: *Put your hands together.*

Stand up, with your backs to each other. Each person spends a little time getting fully aware of themselves and their gifts. When you are ready, turn around to face your partner. Wait patiently until your partner turns around. When both of you have turned around, place your hands together, palms touching. Feel the energy of your palms and your partner's palms. When you have felt that energy, move one step back, your palms no longer touching, but still facing each other. Continue feeling the energy of the other person's palms.

STEP THREE: *Feel the space between.*

After exploring that energy for a while, start feeling the energy not of your partner but of what exists in the connected space between you and your partner. Compare your perceptions with your partner's. How did your partner's energy feel? How did yours feel to you? What was the energy like that you created between the two of you?

USING JUDGMENT

GOAL: *To turn judgments into transformational jumping-off points*

STEP ONE: *Name the judgment.*

Clearly state your projection or judgment. Write it down in your Unfolding Notebook.

STEP TWO: *Feel the judgment.*

Imagine you are in a situation that would bring up this judgment. What else are you feeling, in addition to the judgment? Fear? Anger? Sadness?

STEP THREE: *Switch places.*

Put yourself in the other person's shoes for a moment. What might she be feeling toward you? What might she be feeling toward herself?

STEP FOUR: *Come back to yourself.*
Become yourself again. Ask yourself if there has
ever been a time when you've felt like the person
you've been projecting things onto or judging.
What kind of situation was that? What one thing
would you change that could have made that situation feel better?

STEP FIVE: *Change the judgment.*
Imagine you can change that small thing, in yourself, right now. Imagine the situation again, this
time with the change. Did your change make the
difference you thought it would? If not, go back to
Step Four and choose to change something else.

DIFFERENTIATION

GOAL: *To differentiate between your growth
community and your resonant environment*

STEP ONE: *Pick a nonresonant person.*
Think of someone in your growth community
whom you no longer choose to be with. Imagine
surrounding that person with your light.

STEP TWO: *Ask them to leave.*
In your mind, tell that person why you no longer
wish to include them in your environment. Ask
them if they have anything to ask or say. Listen to
their reply.

STEP THREE: *See them in your growth community.*
Visualize your growth community. Notice all its members, living and dead, including this person. Visualize
this person living his or her life within your growth community, but not in your resonant environment.

STEP FOUR: *See the future without them.*
Now project yourself into the future. Imagine your

environment without this person. See yourself interacting with others in your resonant environment, without this person present. Ask yourself how this vision feels.

STEP FIVE: *Bless them.*

If you can imagine this person within your growth community but not in your resonant environment, commit to making this experience a reality. Write down what you need to do to leave this person with your blessing.

> RITUALS

UNION/SEPARATION

GOAL: *To acknowledge and celebrate an individual's needs in a close relationship, as well as the needs of the relationship itself*

What You'll Need:

- a close (not necessarily romantic) partner
- fifteen minutes in a private space
- an object that both partners agree symbolizes your relationship
- one object that represents you
- one object that represents your partner

1. Spend a minute or so holding hands, facing each other, and being silent. When ready, each partner picks up the object that represents him- or herself. Each partner spends a moment being with the object, and being with him- or herself. Partners can go into separate rooms or do whatever they need to center themselves.

2. Partners come back into the same room. Still
   holding the object, one partner tells the other who
   they are, in the most basic sense, using whatever
   words come. The other partner just listens. Now the
   listener describes him- or herself. When each partner
   has finished, each gives his or her object to the
   other. Hold your partner's object for a while to get
   a full experience of your partner's soul.

3. When you are ready, place the objects aside. Both
   partners pick up the object that represents the
   relationship. Spend a moment feeling the object,
   holding it, listening to it. What does it have to say to
   you about your relationship?

4. Still holding the object together, each partner picks
   up the object that symbolizes her- or himself. Hold
   all three objects together, between you. Each partner might share a blessing for themselves, the
   other person, and the relationship.

TRANSMISSION

GOAL: *To establish a sense of continuity with others
in your growth community*

What You'll Need:

- half an hour to an hour (depending on group size)
- a group of people in your growth community who
  are also in your resonant environment
- shells, rocks, flowers, and/or any other beautiful
  natural objects — at least one for each person
- a private space with a flat surface (the floor will do)

1. Gather the group in a circle. Let each person pick
   one of the natural objects. Let one person start the

ritual by taking his or her object and naming it after their soul's work.

ЄХΛМ Р L Є : A shell could be renamed "music."

2. That person gives the object to another person in the group. The receiver thanks the giver and adds the gift to his or her own. Then the receiver keeps the gift, finds a name for their gift, and gives their gift to another person. In this way, the energy of the first gift is transmitted along with the energy of the second.

3. Each person becomes a receiver of another's gift and a giver of his or her own gift, until the original giver has become a receiver.

4. Spend a few moments talking about how it felt to receive and give the gifts. Did anyone feel afraid to part with her or his gift? Was anyone resisting receiving a gift? Did anyone not want the received gift to influence his or her original gift?

Chapter Six: Creation
MEDITATIONS

"_____ needs me."

(Fill in the blank with the goal of your goal community — a reminder that although you may experience self-transcendence, you must be present as well.)

"I offer my gifts to a healing creation."

(Use this meditation if you are unsure that your goal community is worthwhile. See if it rings true.)

"I choose my goal community."

(This meditation can be useful especially when the members of a goal community get into difficulties, such as personal disagreements.)

"I release my work."

(This meditation supports the sometimes-difficult process of letting go of your soul's work.)

HANDS II

GOAL: *To celebrate the transcendent space among members of a goal community*

STEP ONE: *Gather the members.*

Gather members of your goal community in a circle. All members should keep silent until Step Four, except the member leading the practice.

STEP TWO: *Become aware of yourself.*

Stand up, with your backs to the circle. Each person spends a little time getting fully aware of themselves and their gifts. When ready, turn around to face the circle. Wait patiently until everyone turns around. When everyone has turned around, move on to the next step.

STEP THREE: *Connect with others.*

Hold hands around the circle. Feel the energy of your palms and the palms of the people next to you. When you have felt that energy, let go, your hands no longer touching. Continue feeling the energy of the people next to you. After exploring that energy for a while, start feeling the energy of the others in the circle. Use your hands to reach toward them, if it helps you feel the energy. Feel their strength, uniqueness, and beauty.

STEP FOUR: *Know your creation.*

Begin to explore the energy of the community, the energy that lives in the center of the circle. Let your hands trace its shape, feeling its lumps and bumps, knowing intimately its strong and weak parts. Compare your perceptions with those of the group. How did other people's energy feel? How did yours feel to you? What was the energy like that you created between all of you?

BEGINNING/ENDING

GOAL: *When you feel done with your unfolding work, this practice brings you back through your path as a review, then asks you to start again*

STEP ONE: *Hear your path.*

Imagine your whole path in front of you. Listen to what your path has to say. What would it like you to know? What lessons can it teach you?

STEP TWO: *Get into the whole.*

Fly to the "ocean" part of your path — the part where your energy flows into the pool with the energy of everyone in your goal community — or bigger yet, into the pool with the energy of everyone in the universe. Let yourself come down in the middle of this pool, the place of the whole.

STEP THREE: *Remember wholeness.*

Be in the ocean as the whole, remembering all the love that you, God, and others put into the ocean. Let yourself feel that love as if it is all for you, as if you are the new source that is being created. Bask in that love as long as you like. Imagine dissipating in the ocean, being unable to find where you begin and where anything else ends.

STEP FOUR: *Find your source.*

When you are ready, you may start noticing that you are more attracted to one area of this pool than to any other. Go to that area, and let yourself refocus there. This is your source, beginning to separate out from the whole, so that you may begin again.

STEP FIVE: *Get out of the whole.*

See if you are willing and ready — excited and delighted — to step out and move back into a place where your source is separate. If so, allow yourself to do this in whatever way occurs to you. If not, let yourself remain in the whole until you desire to begin your unfolding again. Record your observations in your Unfolding Notebook.

RITUALS

MEMBERSHIP

GOAL: *To support full participation of new members in a goal community*

What You'll Need:

- about half an hour in a private space
- the new member
- several longstanding members of the goal community
- several long-standing members of the goal community who have recently joined
- one chair

1.   Tell the new member that the center of the circle is the most important position — it is where the goal itself is formed. Ask the new member to sit in the chair while the other members face him or her in a circle.

2.   Each member in the circle says their name and their purpose (as it occurs to them in this moment) as well as the element of the goal that most resonates with them.

3. Once all current members are done, the new
    member is invited to say his or her name and
    purpose and the element of the goal that most
    resonates with them.

4. Ask the new member to think about how he hopes
    to contribute to the community. If he wants to
    speak this hope out loud, that is fine, but it is not
    required. The other members in the circle silently
    accept, the new member and his contribution
    (even if they are unspoken), until one of them
    asks the new member to join the circle.

5. All members join hands and face the empty chair,
    blessing that now-open position for any new mem-
    ber that may bring an important change to the goal
    community.

PARTNERSHIP

GOAL: *To embody within a close relationship the three
essential communities: resonance, growth, and goal*

What You'll Need:

- a close (not necessarily romantic) partner
- fifteen minutes in a private space
- three scarves or pieces of fabric
- a sense of the goals of your relationship

1. Sit, stand, or lie close to your partner. Ask your
    partner if she or he will be in your resonance
    community — use whatever words feel right to you.
    Let your partner answer honestly. Now let your
    partner ask you the same question. Let your-
    self answer honestly. Choose one of the scarves and
    surround you and your partner with it.

Together, visualize yourselves in the same
resonance community.

2. Leaving the scarf in place, ask each other if you will
willingly be in the same growth community. Again,
use the words that seem best to each of you, and
answer only when completely sure. Choose another
scarf and surround you and your partner with it.
Together, visualize yourselves in the same growth
community.

3. Leave both scarves in place. Now ask one another if
you will be in the same goal community.
Remember — you can each have other goal
communities — this goal community is devoted to
the goal of your relationship. Place the final scarf
around you and your partner. Visualize yourselves
working toward your goal together.

4. When you are finished, slowly remove the scarves,
one at a time. As you do, each state a blessing for
your goal, growth, and resonant communities.

PLANTING II

GOAL: *To celebrate the plants that the seeds (from Planting Ritual 1) have become, and so to celebrate your unfolding*

What You'll Need:

- a half hour set aside
- your Unfolding Notebook
- the plants that you planted in Planting Ritual I

1. Return to the place in your Unfolding Notebook where you recorded your responses to the first planting ritual. Look at where you wrote down the needs of the seeds, as well as what you thought you would need for your unfolding. Look at the plants you planted, as well as (in your mind's eye) the path of your unfolding. Were you able to give the seeds and yourself what you needed?

2. Now notice what you recorded you might do if the seeds did not grow, and what you might do if your unfolding was blocked. Did you have the opportunity to try either of these plans? Or did you develop another plan?

3. Now read your notebook entry about your wishes for the seeds and your wishes for your unfolding. Did your wishes come true?

4. Let yourself observe and respond to the plants you have grown. What is beautiful about them? How are they successful? Let yourself feel love for them.

5. Now take in yourself. What is beautiful about you? How are you successful? Let yourself feel love for yourself.

6. What will you plant next time?

ABOUT
Julia Mossbridge

Julia Mossbridge is a thirty-three-year-old mother, biologist, and author. After receiving her master's degree in neuroscience, Julia left a competitive doctorate program at the University of California in San Francisco to understand and pursue her soul's work. During a five-year hiatus from research, she began recording her insights about her own process and that of the others she taught, coached, healed, worked with, and entertained as a workshop leader, life coach, energy healer, technology manager, and radio talk-show cohost.

When she returned to science in 1998, Julia was honored at the World Marine Mammalogy Conference in Monaco for her work on Antarctic killer whale communication. Her essay about first-time motherhood appeared in the 2001 *Hip Mama* anthology, *Breeder*. She has also been seen too many times in an embarrassing MTV segment in which she discusses chlamydia. Julia is the cofounder of Humans in Science, a group of scientists working to bring ethical, environmental, personal, and spiritual concerns into everyday scientific and career decisions. Julia lives in Evanston, Illinois, with her partner and son and attends graduate school at Northwestern University. This is her first book.

THE UNFOLDING WEBSITE, NEWSLETTER, AND WORKSHOP SERIES

Unfolding.org offers experiments, rituals, links, and other resources intended to support personal and community transformation. The *Unfolding Newsletter* (a free monthly e-mail publication) was conceived in August 2000 and reaches hundreds of readers with ideas, stories, exercises, and messages about transformation and world repair. Subscribe at www.unfolding.org.

The Unfolding workshop series began in 1996 and has since taken many forms. The series has two goals: to gently move participants through their own unfolding process and to create a community of people who are committed to healing the world with their gifts. For more information about the series, visit the Unfolding website at www.unfolding.org.